P9-AZV-919

Quick and Dirty

A Compact Guide to
Writing, Reading, and Research

FIFTH EDITION

Fred Cooksey

Crooked Pig Press

Easthampton, Massachusetts

CROOKED PIG PRESS

Easthampton, Massachusetts 01027

413.282.8701

Copyright © 2020 by Fred Cooksey

All rights reserved. No part of this book may be reproduced, stored in a retrieval system, or transmitted in any form or by any means, electronic, mechanical, photocopying, recording, or otherwise, except as may be expressly permitted by the applicable copyright statutes or in writing by the author.

Manufactured in the United States of America.

For Zoe, Betsy, and Mom

https://sites.google.com/view/crookedpigpress

CONTENTS

I FIRST THINGS FIRST

1 COLLEGE SURVIVAL   **1**

What Does a College Degree Mean in America Today?   1
What *Not* to Do in Your College Classes   3
A Few Pieces of Advice   8

2 READING AND CRITICAL THINKING   **10**

Information vs. Opinion   11
Types of Writers   12
Types of Publications   15
How to Spot Fake News   17
Warning: Mind Games Ahead   20
Ethos, Pathos, Logos   22
Active Reading   25

3 COMMON ERRORS   **31**

Commonly Confused Words   32
Common Sentence Errors   38
A Few Rules Worth Learning   46

II WRITING

4 WRITING WITH SOURCES   **54**

Summarizing, Paraphrasing, and Quoting   56
Interacting with Sources   62
Plagiarism   64

5 WRITING A PAPER   **65**

Why Do You Have to Write Papers?   65
Pre-writing   68
Writing a Draft   77
Analytical Writing   78
"I" Statements / First Person: Proceed with Caution   81
Transitions   82
Revising   84
First Impressions   85

6 EDITING & PROOFREADING   **86**

III RESEARCH AND DOCUMENTATION

7   FINDING SOURCES   **95**

Google   96
Google Scholar   104
Library Databases   106
Finding Books   112

8   MLA DOCUMENTATION   **114**

In-Text Citations   116
Works-Cited Entries   129
Sample MLA Student Paper   152

9   APA DOCUMENTATION   **161**

In-Text Citations   162
Reference List Entries   169
Sample APA Student Paper   180

10   STUDENT PAPERS   **193**

Student MLA Longer Paper (5 pages)   194
Student MLA Short Paper (3 pages)   206
Christopher Kobylinksy on Organization   213

APPENDIX : TECHNOLOGY TIPS   **214**

INDEX   **224**

PREFACE

Why is it called *Quick and Dirty*?

You don't hear it much anymore, but people used to say, "Just give me the quick and dirty." It meant: Tell me what I need to know efficiently and without excess explanation. That was my goal in writing this book—to give students the information you need about writing, reading, and research quickly, and in simple terms.

ACKNOWLEDGEMENTS

I would like to thank a number of colleagues and friends for their significant contributions to the changes in this edition, particularly Christopher Kobylinsky, who has offered many wise suggestions and has been willing to read and comment on so much of this new edition.

Further thanks to Marsha Van Duren her insightful and perceptive corrections and musings, and for her incredible attention to detail, especially for her proofreading of Chapters 2, 4, 5, 6, and 7; Andrew Morse for his extensive feedback on sample essays in Chapters 8 and 9, and his eagle-eyed proofreading of Chapter 3; Shelby Kreiger, for her excellent feedback on the first sample essay as well as her close attention to the MLA chapter; Shira Simon, for her ever-careful reading of the APA chapter; Elizabeth Trobaugh for her deep understanding of what students need from this book; Jacqueline Dailey for her no-nonsense practicality, wit, and encouragement; Lisa Mahon for her advice on organization and bigger-picture ideas; Julie Cafritz for her even-quicker-and-dirtier suggestions, and for her advice on introductions and conclusions; and, last but hardly least, Rosemary Kress and Chris Mullen for their outstanding cover design.

And to my many colleagues and friends who have used previous editions of this book in their classes, my deepest gratitude—without you, I would have given up on this years ago.

Finally, thanks to the many students who have offered kind words of encouragement as well as some very useful suggestions.

Fred Cooksey
March 2020

chapter 1

COLLEGE SURVIVAL
OR, WHAT *NOT* TO DO IN YOUR CLASSES

Only the educated are free.
> ~ Epictetus

The more we learn the more we realize how little we know.
> ~ R. Buckminster Fuller

WHAT DOES A COLLEGE DEGREE MEAN IN AMERICA TODAY?

A piece of paper.

That's how students often talk about it, and that—in many ways—is how many employers view it.

Particularly in the world of work, a college degree means that you are able to complete a variety of time-consuming, sometimes demanding, and sometimes tedious tasks. Some of those tasks will require you to apply every ounce of your intelligence, while others will call only on your ability to memorize trivial information that you will probably forget within a matter of hours.

Finishing college may or may not make you smarter, but it will certainly prove that you have discipline. That's one reason employers want people with college degrees. When you complete a degree, it communicates to potential employers,

"I am able to complete many tasks, even when some of them are not interesting to me personally."

That's an admirable personal quality, one that you will find useful in any number of real-life situations.

However. This is a big However. What I just described is what college "represents" in our world. That doesn't mean that college can't—and shouldn't—be much more. It should make you a deeper and more analytical thinker. It should expose you to new ideas that cause you to rethink your understanding of the world. It should allow you to approach intellectual and practical problems in more creative and productive ways. It should make you a better citizen.

As someone who believes in the ability of college to do all of those things (and more), I'm asking you to try to pursue those high-minded ideals. Avoid courses that ask you only to memorize and regurgitate information. Seek out courses that turn your intellectual world upside-down, that confuse and bewilder and challenge you.

It's worth it.

* * *

So here you are in college. Maybe you're eighteen and just out of high school. Or you took some time off to work or have a family. Whoever you are, if you're reading this, it's most likely because you're taking English Composition.

Many students don't exactly look forward to this course, in part because they don't feel confident about their writing. That's why I wrote this book—to make the work you need to do in your first-year writing class easier and less mysterious. Hopefully, the lessons you learn here will also help you with the reading, writing, and research you'll have to do in other classes.

With both English Composition and your other courses in mind, I'll begin with survival skills. Plenty of books suggest "techniques for success," but I find most of the suggestions clichéd: study hard, don't put off assignments till the last minute, take a multivitamin, etc. Instead, I'll tell you what *not* to do. It takes the form of a Top 10 list.

WHAT *NOT* TO DO IN YOUR COLLEGE CLASSES

10. IGNORE THE SYLLABUS

Some students never bother to read the syllabus. I understand—it's annoying that every professor has different policies around absences, grading, phones, late papers, etc. But it's not so different from the real world, where one boss will be lenient and easy-going while another will be strict and demanding.

Do yourself a favor and read the syllabus closely. Your professor will be impressed if you're able to say, for example, "I know that if I turn the paper in Thursday, there will be a half-letter-grade penalty." They* might even be impressed enough to grade your paper a little more generously.

9. COMMUNICATE POORLY

When you need to call or email your professor, think about the language and form you use. Far too many students send emails that look like this:

> hi, i'm in your english class and can't come to school today my mom's car is in the shop and there are no buses around here so let me know what i need to do.

Even if your professor wants you to call them by their first name, you should try to make your language and tone relatively formal. It should not read like a text to one of your friends.

> Dear Professor _____,
>
> I'm in your MWF 10-10:50 English class, and I am unable to come to school today. I will continue to read the essay that's assigned on the syllabus, but if there's anything else I should do, please let me know. Thank you very much.
>
> Sincerely,
>
> Joe Student

---

* Please see page 44 for my approach to using *they, them, and their* in constructions like this.

A few basic guidelines: Use capital letters, as you would in a paper for class. Write in complete sentences. Thank the person you're writing to. Include a "closing," e.g., *Sincerely*, or *Kind regards*, or *Best*. Proofread what you've written.

Take the same approach to phone messages. Speak clearly, say your phone number slowly, and thank the person you're calling.

Finally, try not to bombard your professor with email or phone messages. Many of us teach a hundred or more students, and if we have to respond to 20 or 30 student emails a day (a common occurrence for some professors), it amounts to a lot of time that we're not able to use for grading, finding new materials for class, and so on.

8. TALK WHILE PROFESSOR IS TALKING

Rude, disrespectful.

7. COME TO CLASS WITHOUT BOOK(S), PAPER, PEN, ETC.

Makes you look like you don't care. And maybe you don't. But that certainly won't reflect well on you when we're grading your papers and tests. I could pretend that we grade everything "in a vacuum," which is to say without thinking about who you are as a person in the classroom. But that would be a lie. It's like anything else in life—you're always making an impression on the people around you. What will yours be?

Related: Try to approach the classroom with a sense of "professionalism," as if it were a job and the professor is your boss. If your professor writes something on the board, for example, that means it's pretty important. So it's probably a good idea for you to write it down.

6. NOT READ OR FOLLOW DIRECTIONS

You'll sometimes have assignments with very specific directions or multiple steps to follow. Read closely and don't assume you know what's being asked of you without paying close attention.

Sometimes you'll find certain directions confusing. In that case, it's fine to ask for clarification from your professor, but be sure to first give it your best effort. Don't just skim the instructions and then say you don't know what to do.

What I'm really asking you to try to develop in yourself is self-reliance and discipline. These are traits that will serve you well in all aspects of life beyond college.

5. PACK UP PAPERS AND BOOKS BEFORE CLASS IS OVER

Rude, rude, rude—both to the professor and your classmates. It's noisy and distracting. When you do this, you are communicating to all who can see or hear you, "I have declared this class to be finished."

Relax.

4. COME TO CLASS LATE / LEAVE CLASS (EARLY)

Once class is in session, any movement around the room is going to be distracting. If you're late, find a seat as quickly and quietly as you can. Try to avoid walking in front of the class—it's often best to take a seat near the door rather than walking through the room. If you know in advance that you have to leave before the end of class, talk to the professor in advance.

Moving around during class is pretty distracting too. Increasingly, I see students simply get up and walk out of class, casually, and return a few minutes later. Maybe they're going to the bathroom—which is fine if it's a legitimate need but not so fine if the class is only 50 minutes long. Sometimes I see students get up in the middle of a discussion to throw away a piece of paper. It can wait. Other times, I know they're stepping outside to make a phone call. Is anything really that important that it couldn't wait till class is over?

In short, try to be a "good citizen" within class. You're in a shared learning environment, and your behavior has an impact on everyone around you.

3. ASK THE PROFESSOR "DID I MISS ANYTHING?" AFTER AN ABSENCE

Yes, of course! The question seems to assume that there might be days when nothing of importance happens during class, an implication that many of your professors would be a little offended by.

Rephrasing it as "What did I miss?" is an improvement, but before you ask this, think about how you might avoid the question altogether. If the course syllabus includes a calendar of assignments, look there to see what you missed. You might also ask a classmate if you can copy (or photograph) their notes.

If you still have questions, talk to the professor during office hours. But don't expect us to go over everything we did. We'll give you a brief summary of the subject(s) we covered, and then it's your responsibility to figure out how to learn that material. This is true even if you had an excellent reason for missing class. We simply can't recreate a 50- or 75-minute class for every student who's absent.

2. SKIP REQUIRED READING

More and more often, it seems, students are coming to class without having done assigned reading. Maybe they figure the professor will be "going over" that article or chapter, so there's no point in reading it in advance.

Here's the irony of this development. For the last twenty or so years, professors have been encouraged to lecture less and involve students in classroom discussions more. Many of us have moved in this direction, but now, when we try to have an actual discussion of a reading, it often falls flat because many students haven't done the reading.

In terms of being educated, there's nothing more important than reading. Not browsing, not checking *SparkNotes*, not googling a summary—just good old-fashioned reading.

1. BECOME DISTRACTED / BECOME A DISTRACTION

If you're using a phone or some other electronic device during class, you're not giving the professor—or your classmates—your full attention. I don't allow laptops in my classes, though I may have to rethink this prohibition at some point. I recognize that laptops can be beneficial in a variety of ways (note-taking, vocabulary, fact-checking, etc.), but I also know that many students aren't using them to augment what's going on in class; they're using them to *escape* what's going on in class. They're checking Instagram or Snapchat or their fantasy football league, shopping for shoes, applying for jobs. All fun and even useful things to do. But not during class, please.

Of course, some students will argue that if a class is boring, then what's the harm in escaping for a few minutes? But the harm is not to you—it's to me and your classmates, many of whom are aware of what you're doing and are distracted by it.

I love the Internet. I spend far too much time on it, and not much of it is well-spent, so I'm not judging you. But I am asking you to consider how your decision to entertain yourself during class may affect the people around you as well as your professor.

Even if your professor doesn't have a stated policy about phones or laptops, I would encourage you to try to be electronics-free during class. There's a lot to be said for the old-fashioned approach of taking hand-written notes and simply being fully *present* for your education.

(Have a look at the student essays—offering competing views on this topic—at the end of Chapters 8 and 9.)

A FEW PIECES OF ADVICE THAT DIDN'T FIT INTO THE TOP 10

Take advantage of the Writing Center

Whether you're an experienced, confident writer or one who's struggling, you'll find a visit to the Writing Center will almost always make your paper better. In order to get the most out of your time with a writing tutor, be sure to bring the assignment with you. Also, it's best if you do at least some of the writing before your visit. A tutor can help you with planning, but you give them more to work with if you have a draft—or at least an outline.

Writing Center tutors are also available online. Go to your college's Writing Center page to find the link to online tutoring.

Choose your classes wisely

When it's time to sign up for the next semester of classes, try to make choices based on more than just convenient scheduling—although it is smart to avoid, say, 8 a.m. classes if you know you're going to struggle to be on time and alert for the class.

Ask your classmates about the courses they loved (or hated), and definitely try to find out which professors are well regarded. Also remember that the first week of the semester is an "add-drop" period when you can make changes. If you immediately sense that you're not going to be able to learn from a particular professor, see if there's another section of the same course you can take.

I remember the first day of a political science course my freshman year, when I immediately found the professor unfriendly and difficult (not in terms of intellect but personality). I thought, *Oh, well, I'll just deal with it.* I dealt with it, but never happily—I had a miserable time in that class and learned almost nothing. After that, I started reading the course evaluations that were available in the library, and I quickly learned which professors to avoid.

Plan ahead

In the syllabus for most courses, you'll find a calendar of readings, exams, and major assignments. You might not know the exact date for each of these, but you should know at least what week you'll have work due. You need to know if you have two five-page papers and an exam all due at the end of seventh week. You'll want to get started ahead of time on at least one of those papers.

Sometimes it's smart to ask for an extension on a paper due date. The professor might say no, but it's always worth asking. Explain your circumstances—and maybe show your professor the due dates for the other work. Bear in mind that most professors are unlikely to give an extension if you ask for it the day before a paper is due.

How to ask for a letter a letter of recommendation

If you plan to transfer to another college, you'll probably need at least one letter of recommendation. If you're not sure which professor(s) to ask, start with the courses where you did well (obviously). If you took more than one course with a professor, that's someone you should consider asking because they know your work in multiple contexts and can write a more thorough evaluation of your strengths and weaknesses.

Ask for the recommendation as far in advance as possible—two weeks or more if possible.

If you're applying to a school that uses the Common Application, it's pretty straightforward: You put your professor's email address in the application, and the Common App sends him/her a link to fill out the recommendation. Some smaller schools have a different process, so find out what's involved before you speak to your professor.

If you plan to ask a professor for a letter of recommendation via email (acceptable but not as good as doing it in person), triple-check everything in your message—and maybe have a friend look it over quickly to see if you missed any obvious errors. You don't want your writing there to reflect poorly on you just before the professor writes the recommendation.

I think it's smart to send your professor a thank-you note (via email is fine) after the recommendation has been submitted. Professors aren't compelled to write recommendations, and it does take some time, so sending us a quick thank you is a nice thing to do. And of course we'll want to know if you got into the college of your dreams, so send us an email to tell us that too. Your success is a large part of what makes our work feel important and valuable.

QD

chapter 2

READING & CRITICAL THINKING

Too often we give students answers to remember rather than problems to solve.

~ Roger Lewin

All of us show bias when it comes to what information we take in. We typically focus on anything that agrees with the outcome we want.

~ Noreena Hertz

All writing is rhetorical. This is a popular saying among English teachers. What it means is that writers are always trying to get the reader to see things their way. I'm challenging you, in this chapter, to think about how writers make rhetorical decisions that—they hope—will cause you to agree with the "world" they're presenting in their writing.

In college, you'll be asked to read three basic types of writing: **informative**, **opinion-based**, and **literary**. The difference between informative and opinion-based writing may seem obvious, but often it isn't—mainly because many writers who are trying to get you to see things their way are good at blurring the lines between fact and opinion. So, even when you're reading an article or essay that appears to be plainly informative, you should be aware of how the writer may be "positioned" on a particular issue. In other words, they may have a stance or point of view that they want you to accept.

INFORMATION VS. OPINION VS. LITERATURE

Information

- Some textbooks
  - › math and many science textbooks are generally factual in their presentation of material
- Newspaper and magazine news
  - › should not offer an opinion or view on the news (but often does)
- Encyclopedias, dictionaries, and other reference works
  - › Wikipedia is generally reliable but will often have inaccurate or misleading information

Opinion (also known as persuasion, argument, commentary, interpretation, analysis)

- Many textbooks
  - › textbooks in history and political science / government are increasingly interpretive—scholars often don't agree about "what happened" in the past, or on what many historical events mean
- Many articles that appear in news feeds
  - › they may look like "news reports," but they frequently contain bias and/or opinion
- Most nonfiction books
  - › even those that rely largely on facts are also simultaneously interpreting or analyzing those facts
  - › most are "positioned" in one way or another: they provide information and/or research but present it in a specific way to influence how you feel about the subject matter
- Almost all scholarly / journal articles
  - › see Chapter 7 (Finding Sources) for more on analyzing scholarly writing

Literature (fiction: novels, short stories; poetry, drama/plays, creative nonfiction)

- › creative works often resemble real life, but all are the invention of their authors
- › historical fiction is usually a blend of actual history and invention/fictionalizing

TYPES OF WRITERS

WHO ARE YOU READING?

You'll have an advantage in understanding what you read if you know more about some different types of writers—and what their differences mean for you as a reader. For example, let's say you read this sentence somewhere online:

Eating cereal for breakfast is far healthier than eating nothing.

Fine, you think—that sounds reasonable. Your first instinct is to believe the statement. But who wrote it? The author's name (I'm making this up to illustrate a point) is Jason Yost. You've never heard of him.

Now, how would you feel about that piece of "information" if Jason Yost were

- a researcher in nutrition science at Yale University
- a part-time blogger for the website *Love Cereal*
- the president of a company that owns five major cereal manufacturers

The answer makes a huge difference in how we interpret the information. This is primarily because of two factors: motivation and qualification.

MOTIVATION

Both the Yale researcher and the blogger might be motivated by the search for truth; both might desire to advance our understanding of nutrition.

But the company president is most likely motivated by the desire to sell more cereal. Whatever "the truth" might be, the company president is far more likely to manipulate it so that it serves his needs.

QUALIFICATION

Like many things in life, this is not an "either-or" question. Think of it instead as being on a continuum, like this:

Not at all qualified   Somewhat qualified   Highly qualified

←———————|————————————|————————————|————————→

In our example, the Yale researcher is highly qualified, the blogger is probably not at all qualified, and the company president—who knows? You'd have to find out about his credentials.

Sometimes it's not so simple to determine what kind of writer you're reading, so I'll describe some of the basic types you're likely to encounter. In case it's not confusing enough, keep in mind that not all writers fit neatly into these categories. For example, a writer might be a scholar when they publish papers and books about marine biology—but when they publish an opinion piece in a newspaper or magazine, they're both a scholar and an opinion writer.

REPORTERS / JOURNALISTS

Reporters typically work for newspapers and magazines. Generally, they are not specialists in any particular field—rather, they know how to gather information (usually via interviews, but also through primary sources like government documents) and put it together in a way that can be understood by a broad audience. It's also true, though, that at the best newspapers, most reporters are extremely knowledgeable about more specific areas: Congress, the automotive industry, education, football, etc.

OPINION WRITERS

When you read the works of opinion writers, it's important to distinguish between those who are "generalists" and those who are "experts." Most opinion writers are generalists—meaning that they typically write about a range of issues, none of which they are "expert" in. For example, a newspaper columnist might write an essay about global warming—and it might be quite well researched and persuasive—even though they never did formal academic work in environmental science, geology, or meteorology.

Sometimes, opinion writers *are* experts. Look for a biographical note about the author that explains who the person is. For example, I recently read an opinion essay about a legal controversy. At the end of the essay, the biographical note about the writer said this: "John Farmer, a former attorney general of New Jersey and senior counsel to the 9/11 commission, teaches at Rutgers Law School." In other words, the author is an expert on law. It doesn't mean he's right, of course—but it does mean that he should know matters of law that a generalist might not.

SCHOLARS

Scholars have been educated (usually through the PhD level) in a specific field, such as sociology, philosophy, English, physics, and so on. Furthermore, most PhD-level work is highly specialized, with the scholar focused on a particular part of their field. For example, a PhD student in biology might focus on cellular and molecular biology, with a further specialization in food safety.

When you read a scholar writing in their field, you should expect to encounter a high level of language and perhaps some jargon specific to the field. There will likely be numerous references to other research done in the field, as well as footnotes and/or endnotes and a bibliography.

PROFESSIONAL WRITERS

That word *professional* might not be the best choice—but I want it to convey that the writer is an employee, typically of a company or organization. Unlike a reporter, the professional writer's goal is not (necessarily) to tell the truth; instead, it's to depict the company or organization in the most flattering light. This doesn't necessarily mean that the writer is going to lie to you. But it's frequently the case that these writers stretch, twist, and manipulate facts so that the reader will be sympathetic to the company or organization.

Sometimes you'll find these writers in reputable publications, which may make you think that the writer is credible (believable). Always look for more information about the author. For example, if a biographical note tells you the author is "the director of security for Giant Computer Systems," you should read the article/essay with the understanding that the author's first allegiance is not to you, the reader, or to "the truth," but to the organization that pays their salary. When in doubt, do a quick Google search for the author to find out where they work.

TYPES OF PUBLICATIONS

Now that you know something about the types of writers you're likely to encounter, you should know something about the publications you might find them in. See Chapter 7 (Finding Sources) for more information.

- Newspapers
- Scholarly journals
- Magazines
- Books
- "Elite" magazines

NEWSPAPERS

Newspapers have played an important role in our country's history, but in recent years they have come under attack from both sides of the political divide. Major newspapers have certainly made mistakes, and it's also true that you can often detect bias in how they report on some people and events. Still, they have an important responsibility to tell readers what's happening in the world—and to question those in power, no matter their political affiliation. News organizations may not get it right 100% of the time, and they may sometimes seem to attack people you like, but they remain a vital part of our democracy.

Detail from an illustration that appeared in *Puck* magazine, 1894.

In 1787, thirteen years before he would become the second president of the United States, Thomas Jefferson wrote, "Were it left to me to decide whether we should have a government without newspapers or newspapers without a government, I should not hesitate a moment to prefer the latter."

In other words, he had a strong belief that newspapers were a better safeguard of people's rights than the government itself.

Now, in fairness, I should add that Jefferson had a very different take on newspapers twenty years later, when he was nearing the end of his second term as president. In an 1807 letter to a friend, he wrote:

"I will add, that the man who never looks into a newspaper is better informed than he who reads them; inasmuch as he who knows nothing is nearer to truth than he whose mind is filled with falsehoods & errors."

In case that's not immediately clear to you, he was saying that someone who never read a newspaper was closer to truth than the person who did read them. Then again, newspapers in that period were well known for their very personal attacks on politicians, and this trend continued throughout the 1800s; it reached its peak late in the 1800s, when the term "yellow journalism" came into being. That term described the way that newspapers often published "news" that was little more than gossip, most of it meant to shock rather than inform. The goal was to sell papers and make money for the owner, not to provide useful information to the public. Most newspapers at the time were the BuzzFeed of their day.

In the early 1900s, American journalism went through significant changes; that period is known as "professionalization," and the value of neutrality in reporting became the norm. It meant that the news would be reported in the same way regardless of how the owner of the paper leaned politically.

One of the most important developments of this period was that profit motives became separated from journalistic principles. This also led to key parts of the newspaper becoming separate; the major divisions are news, opinion, and advertising. Typically, those three departments remain completely separate from each other—you wouldn't want, for example, the advertising department to say to the news department, "Don't run that story on contaminated beef; we have $100,000 worth of beef advertising this month."

Interested in learning more about fake news—or do you want to find out if something you heard or read is accurate? Try this site:

FACTCHECK.ORG® *A Project of The Annenberg Public Policy Center*

MAGAZINES

What I call popular, or general-interest, magazines are those that have large circulations and are read by a wide range of people. As with newspapers, most of the articles in these magazines are written by reporters. But you will also find plenty of opinion writing—so you need to be able to tell the two apart.

HOW TO SPOT FAKE NEWS

CONSIDER THE SOURCE

Click away from the story to investigate the site, its mission and its contact info.

READ BEYOND

Headlines can be outrageous in an effort to get clicks. What's the whole story?

CHECK THE AUTHOR

Do a quick search on the author. Are they credible? Are they real?

SUPPORTING SOURCES?

Click on those links. Determine if the info given actually supports the story.

CHECK THE DATE

Reposting old news stories doesn't mean they're relevant to current events.

IS IT A JOKE?

If it is too outlandish, it might be satire. Research the site and author to be sure.

CHECK YOUR BIASES

Consider if your own beliefs could affect your judgement.

ASK THE EXPERTS

Ask a librarian, or consult a fact-checking site.

IFLA
International Federation of Library Associations and Institutions
With thanks to www.FactCheck.org

If you're considering using popular magazines such as *Time, Newsweek* and *U.S. News & World Report* as sources for a paper, be aware that they are not highly respected in the academic world. As background information to help you understand the basics of a topic that is unfamiliar to you, these magazines are fine. But if you're looking for depth of analysis, you won't find it here.

"ELITE" MAGAZINES

"Elite" is a category I created because I believe these sources differ in important ways from popular magazines.

First, though, the similarities; like popular magazines, the elites

- can be found in grocery stores and bookstores
- are for-profit, with their main source of revenue from advertising
- are published weekly, bi-weekly, or monthly

Now, the differences are important, and they have to do mainly with the way the elites cover the news and issues of the day. Elite publications

- print longer articles that go into far more depth
- cover issues that are more complex and less focused on entertainment
- use language that is more sophisticated

While these publications do not have the same standing as scholarly journals, they tend to be respected. However, be aware that most of these publications do have some kind of political bias. Here are some of the magazines that I would include in this group:

The New Yorker	*The New York Times Magazine*
The Atlantic	*The Economist*
Harper's Magazine	*The Nation*
Reason	*National Review*

SCHOLARLY JOURNALS

No matter what field you're in, you're going to have to read scholarly journals, so you should understand something about why they're so important to the academic world. First, though, here's how they're different from magazines:

- Almost all are published by a college or university.
- Most do not accept advertising.

- Articles tend to be less timely than those in magazines and newspapers.
- Few include images or photographs.
- All of the writing is done by scholars in a specific field.
- The primary audience is other scholars in that field.
- Many of the articles use language and/or jargon specific to the field.

What this means is that journal articles will typically be challenging to read, particularly early in your college experience.

Only one other piece of information is important to know about journals before you start using them, and that is that they fall into two categories, those that are peer-reviewed and those that are not. Peer-reviewed journals are the most trusted and reliable sources available. "Peer-reviewed" means that experts in the field (for example, leading scholars of abnormal psychology for the *Journal of Abnormal Psychology*) read and review all articles before they are published. These reviewers tend to be extremely picky about how arguments are constructed and evidence is presented. As a result, peer-reviewed journal articles are some of the most trustworthy sources you can find.

This is not to say that their content will be absolutely *true*. It only means that they shouldn't contain any blatant errors or misrepresentations of fact.

TIP **Pay attention to the first and last paragraphs (and abstracts).** Most essays will reveal their purpose in the first paragraph or two, and often return to it in the final paragraph. Most scholarly articles will also include an abstract, which is a brief summary of the article that appears before the article itself. Note: Some essays will begin by telling a story or doing something slightly unconventional, but in these cases the paragraphs that follow will state the purpose more clearly.

BOOKS

Everyone knows what books are. But how do they fit into this discussion? In some ways, they are a combination of all the categories I've just covered. They can be scholarly, they can be entertaining, they can be trashy. The biggest difference is down to scope: Books allow authors many more pages in which to do their work, so they can go into far more depth.

One more issue for you to be aware of: Books are either fiction or nonfiction. Fiction means that the story has been invented by the author; nonfiction works are true—though that doesn't mean that they're always right or that all readers will agree with the information they present.

For more information on finding books in the library, see pages 112 - 113.

WARNING: MIND GAMES AHEAD

PASSIVE VOICE

Mistakes were made.
> ~ Presidents Reagan, Bush (senior), Clinton, Bush (younger)

Passive is the opposite of active. Grammatically, this means that the writer switches the subject and the object in a sentence, which forces the verb to change:

Active: The boy hit the ball.   Passive: The ball was hit by the boy.

In active voice, the "true" subject (the boy) of the sentence is first, and it performs the action. This is the most common way of forming sentences in the English language. When you switch to passive voice, the meaning is exactly the same, at least in this example. But it's a less natural way for us to read the information. That's the main reason to avoid passive voice as a writer. (Note: I'm not saying you should never use passive voice—only that you should know that you're doing it, and do it for a good reason.)

Sometimes, writers use passive voice because it allows them to omit the "true" subject, the person or thing doing the action, as is the case in the quote above: "Mistakes were made." This statement has become famous—and something of a joke among people who follow politics and/or language—because it has been used by many of our recent presidents to avoid taking responsibility. It should make us ask, *By whom* were mistakes made? But often we don't.

In short, passive voice is not just a grammatical issue—it's also an *ethical* one; here's an example that's closer to your world:

Passive: Tuition and fees at the college were raised.

In the passive voice, the sentence omits an important piece of information: *who* is responsible for the increase in tuition and fees. As a result, we don't know whom to blame—or maybe it never even occurs to us to wonder who's responsible for the increase. Consider the difference when you use active voice:

Active: The college's Board of Trustees raised tuition and fees.

Now we know whom to blame for those increased costs.

Pay attention to how politicians and businesses use language (particularly when they are doing something *to* us), and you'll see that they love the passive voice because it allows them to imply that things simply happen, and that no one has caused them to happen.

EVASIVE LANGUAGE: THE ETHICS OF COMMUNICATION

In the example below, you can certainly figure out what's being said. But it takes some effort. This is the first part of an actual letter from the Massachusetts Division of Insurance a friend of mine received recently:

Original	Upon review of the governing laws and regulations, the evidence presented, and in consideration of the appellant's appeal, it is the determination of the Hearing Officer that the appellant did demonstrate a showing necessary to rebut the governing presumption of the applicable standard of fault.
Translation	You appealed the original Insurance Board finding that you were at fault in the accident on Dec. 15, 2019. Your appeal was successful and we have declared you not at fault in the accident.

The original above is classic *legalese*—the language of lawyers and judges. Personally, I find it offensive that a government body (the Division of Insurance) is allowed to communicate with ordinary citizens in this way. I'm not sure what they have against clear, direct language, but I have a guess: It keeps lawyers in business because ordinary people simply can't make sense of legal jargon. But it's not just jargon—it's the way they structure sentences like the one above. It's such a mess grammatically that it's almost impossible to follow. As the heading on this page says, that—to me—is unethical.

THE LESSON

Be alert to the complex ways in which writers try to manipulate you. It will help you become a better student—and a better citizen.

ETHOS, PATHOS, LOGOS

These words go back to the Greek philosopher Aristotle, who used them to describe how speakers attempt to persuade their audience. They remain useful today in order to help us understand how writers (and speakers) try to influence our thinking. I'll come back to these terms in Chapter 4, and you should think about how you can apply the concepts to your writing as well as your reading.

ETHOS

Writers employ *ethos* when they want you to view them as trustworthy, respected, and believable. Authors don't always need to inject ethos into their writing because their degrees and/or titles do that work for them. Often you'll find these academic credentials in biographical notes about an author (in newspaper and magazine articles). For example, after an article about why people wear face masks during a deadly virus, the biographical note says: "Christos Lynteris is a medical anthropologist at the University of St. Andrews, Scotland." In short, she is uniquely qualified to write about the subject matter of the essay.

In scholarly works, writers communicate their trustworthiness first through the research that they cite. When you see that they've mentioned many of the studies that have been done on the subject of their research, you know that they are well-informed about the knowledge and views that already exist. In the social sciences and hard sciences, writers take great care to describe the methods they use to conduct experiments (also known as *methodology*).

PATHOS

Pathos is an emotional appeal, one that is meant to evoke a range of feelings, including sympathy, sadness, anger, pleasure, and so on. For example, consider this article about students struggling to pay college loan debt. It begins this way:

> Allyssa Gniadek doesn't know whether to laugh or cry when she pages through her pile of student loan financial documents.
>
> "I mean, look at these," she expresses with a loud sigh.
>
> In the eight years since graduating college, the sales manager has paid more than $58,000 on her student loans. However, less than half of that has put a dent in the principal she owes, a balance that still looms at more than $47,000.

"I have so much regret about not educating myself more on what it was going to cost me in the long run to have a degree," Gniadek said.

Allyssa Gniadek celebrates her graduation from UMass-Amherst.

The 30-year-old thought she was making the affordable choice by pursuing a degree from an in-state school like UMass Amherst.

But shortly after donning the cap and gown, the bills for $76,000 in federal and private loans arrived. Before long, the monthly payment had ballooned to $1,100. . . .

The article then shifts away from Gniadek to discuss the hundreds of thousands of other students who may have been victimized by "predatory" loans. By then, though, the article has already built a great deal of sympathy for Gniadek—and many others like her—by focusing our attention on *her* story. It humanizes the issue and makes us much more inclined to believe that student loan debt is a serious problem. The photograph is classic *pathos* in action—there she is, young and happy, freshly graduated from college, just before she realizes exactly how much her debt will damage her financial future.

Pathos is an important technique in advertising and political speech, and it's one that you should train yourself to be aware of. It's not *always* manipulative, but it often is.

LOGOS

Logos is a rational, logical appeal, one that depends on reason and facts. Here's another part of the same article about Allyssa Gniadek that reads very differently from the opening:

> Allegations like that are central to lawsuits filed by five state attorneys general in California, Washington, Pennsylvania, Illinois and Mississippi.
>
> In early 2017, the Consumer Financial Protection Bureau (CFPB) brought a federal case, which claimed Navient "systematically and illegally failed borrowers at every stage of repayment."
>
> Formerly part of Sallie Mae, Navient services the loans of more than 12 million borrowers, including an estimated 225,000 people in Massachusetts. Altogether, it handles more than $300 billion in federal and private student loans.
>
> Along with complaints about forbearance, the lawsuit also accused Navient of incorrectly processing payments, deceiving borrowers about requirements to release a co-signer, and harmed the credit of disabled borrowers.

The seriousness of the allegations against Navient gives the reader an entirely different—and far less emotional—understanding of the issue being brought up in the article. In the excerpt above, the author provides specific figures regarding the number of people affected and the amount of money involved. Those are facts, and they are persuasive to most readers even where emotional appeals might not be. For example, some readers might respond to Allyssa Gniadek's story by saying, "Well, she knew what she was signing; she should have been more careful." But even those readers might be inclined to believe that "predatory" loans are a problem when they see how many young people have been affected by them.

Finally, there's an element of *ethos* present in this section too—the fact that the Consumer Financial Protection Bureau (rather than, say, a single law firm) has brought the suit gives extra weight and credibility to the legal issue.

ACTIVE READING

Life is full of distractions, and it's harder than ever to focus on something you need to read. This section will give you some strategies for reading more actively—in other words, with a sense of purpose. As you read, you have two main goals:

1. *Understand* what the author is saying. In part, this means keeping track of the sources the author uses and what each of them thinks about the subject matter, especially when those sources have conflicting views.

2. *Think critically* about what you're reading. I'll explain this further and illustrate in my notes on the pages opposite the article itself.

Over the next few pages, you'll see excerpts of a news article that appeared recently in the *Washington Post*. To the right of the article you can see my annotations. I keep these notes simple, reducing the content down to the fewest words possible. I often use symbols and abbreviations, and you should do the same. Mostly I'm summarizing what's there, but sometimes I'll "interact" with the source material, usually to question what an author is saying. See page 62 for how this can connect to your writing. The work you do in your annotations will make writing your paper easier.

If the article is important for class discussion or your research, you may want to write more detailed annotations. One advantage of the shorter notes I have here is that I can reconstruct the entire (long) article at a glance just by skimming through my notes.

A few thoughts about my "critical thinking" notes on pages 27 & 29. As soon as I'm sure I understand what the author is saying, I start to ask myself if the writer is trying to influence how I feel about the subject matter. Does the writer emphasize certain information (that fits with how he/she sees the subject matter) while de-emphasizing other information that might contradict or complicate the author's view? How is the article organized—are there important questions or complications that get buried in the middle or not given much attention? What's the tone? In other words, how does the writer *sound* (imagine you're talking to him/her—what facial expressions and gestures would he/she be making?)? Finally, if you're inclined to agree with the writer, try to read the article from the perspective of a person who would come to very different conclusions about the same information. For those moments below, I'll write *Devil's advocate*.

More students are learning on laptops and tablets in class. Some parents want to hit the off switch.

By Debbie Truong

Feb. 1, 2020

1   Meaghan Edwards had just finished reading children's books to her son's third-grade class when the teacher announced that students could have free time before lunch. Instead of playing cards, talking with friends or reading more, the students pulled out their iPads.

parent anti-tech

2   "They were zoned out like little zombies," recalled Edwards, whose children attended school in the Eanes Independent School District in Austin.

3   The school system is one of many coast to coast that have spent millions of dollars on initiatives aimed at putting computers or tablets in the hands of every student, sometimes as early as kindergarten.

schools & tech

4   The largest school district in Virginia, Fairfax County Public Schools, announced last year plans to provide Dell laptops to students starting in third grade. Less wealthy school systems have issued bonds to purchase devices, borrowing millions of dollars for laptops, iPads and Chromebooks.

5   But some parents in parts of the country where the programs are in place want to scale back, saying the devices are harming the way young children learn.

Main idea tech hurts kids

6   From Northern Virginia to Shawnee, Kan., to Norman, Okla., parents have demanded schools reduce or eliminate use of digital devices, provide alternative "low-screen" classwork and allow parents to say they do not want their children glued to glowing screens. Some families have even transferred their children to schools that are not so smitten with technology.

lang.— "smitten"

. . . (skipping paragraphs 7 & 8)

continued on page 28

THINKING CRITICALLY

1   The opening paragraph starts with a brief story about a parent and some third-grade students. Why start this way? To *humanize* the information and make readers sympathetic to Meaghan Edwards (and her son). I notice too that the writer makes a point of naming the things the kids are *not* doing—all things many people would say kids should be doing more of.

2   The quote from the mother is meant to have an impact on the reader; it plays on many people's fears of technology turning people (children!) into "zombies."

3   The third paragraph shifts into a more neutral, unbiased tone. This is an important technique because it lulls the reader into thinking that this article is simple reporting on these events without also commenting on them. However, the end of the last sentence ("as early as kindergarten") seems designed to shock readers and cause concern.

4   Like the previous paragraph, this one comes across as essentially factual. The point is: Many school districts have placed a high priority on providing technology to students. It seems clear that many parents (and the author of this article) will want to question this spending.

    Devil's advocate: Even wealthy school districts have students from poor families; therefore, it's necessary to provide devices to *all* children so that poor students aren't at a disadvantage relative to their wealthier peers.

5   This is what journalists call the "nut graph." In an article like this that doesn't start with "the news" but instead uses a story, this is the paragraph that tells what the actual news is. Is it free from bias? More or less, yes. It appears to be a fact that some parents want to see less technology in their kids' classrooms.

6   This paragraph starts with relatively factual statements meant to show that these concerns are not limited to one school district. The writer's tone comes through in her use of the word "smitten," which means strong affection—but it also suggests a kind of foolishness, as if the affection is not based in rational decision-making.

9 Many parents fear that time spent on screens is eroding the quality of classroom instruction, causing skills such as math and handwriting to atrophy. Others worry that laptops and tablets are damaging children's eyes and posture. And others have shared stories about students viewing pornographic or other inappropriate material on school-issued devices.

concerns -tech

10 They wonder what is lost when so much of childhood is spent staring at a screen instead of conversing with classmates or spending time more creatively. They say that schools are usurping the authority of parents who may limit screen time at home or monitor their children's Internet activity on personal devices.

who's in control

11 In March, Edwards was called to her 6-year-old son's school after other students reported seeing scantily clad and topless women on her son's iPad in class. Her son and a friend, she said, had taken screen shots and saved images of the "naked ladies that they liked" to their devices.

kids + porn

12 A spokeswoman for the Eanes Independent School District said the school system added more Internet security measures after the incident with Edwards's son.

security

. . . (skipping paragraphs 13 - 20)

21 Nowadays, school systems are more likely to argue that providing students with computers is necessary for developing everyday skills. In communities where laptops are used for standardized testing, educators say students must acclimate to the devices to prepare for exams.

naysayer why tech needed

22 Research on the effects of computers and tablets on learning is far from conclusive. A 2015 report found that countries making large investments in technology showed no improvements on student performance in reading, math or science.

tech = no effect?

23 But a Michigan State University researcher found that when school systems properly supported initiatives providing students with computers, higher test scores resulted.

naysayer higher scores

. . .

9   That first line, starting with "Many parents fear," is at the heart of this news story. It lists many of the major concerns and fears parents have.

Devil's advocate: Is there research showing that having access to technology is causing lower math scores? Have those scores even dropped? If so, are there other explanations for the decline? Also—parents fear plenty of things regarding their children's lives, but this doesn't necessarily mean that their objections are reasonable. Also, how many parents are we talking about? The article mentions a few, but the reporter never allows other parents with different views to have a voice.

10 Two paragraphs in a row specifically list parents' concerns, but the author doesn't let us hear from parents who have a different view. Did the author not hear anything positive from any parent about technology in the school system? That seems a little hard to believe—which is starting to make me feel that I'm being manipulated. . . .

11 This paragraph is meant to shock the reader, and it's pretty effective at that. No one likes the idea of a 6-year-old getting access to pornography at school.

12 Here (and in one additional paragraph I haven't included), the author does reveal that the school district took the pornography incident seriously—and apparently did something about it immediately. But she immediately returns to the parent, Edwards, who says she and her husband want to sell their house and move out of the school district (in paragraph 14).

21 As my annotation says, this paragraph functions as a kind of naysayer (see page 80); the author briefly provides the reasons why most school districts embrace technology in the classroom. However, she chooses not to "humanize" these views—no parent or school official is quoted explaining the good that they see in technology.

22 This paragraph seems designed to invalidate the previous paragraph.

23 Finally, a real naysayer! The author knows she can't just attack technology for the entire article—she has to include the "other side." But it takes her 23 paragraphs to get to it, and in the paragraphs that follow she does nothing to address this complication (that computers *can* be beneficial).

Summing up

For the record, I have my own concerns about elementary school students spending too much school time on laptops and tablets—so I mostly agree with the concerns expressed by parents and others in the article.

In spite of this, though, I often found myself questioning the way the writer constructed the article, and I frequently felt that she was not adequately addressing legitimate uses of those technological tools and the ways in which they can help young people learn more effectively. In short, I often felt manipulated by the writer.

If you take nothing else away from this section, I hope you'll remember to think critically about everything you read—*especially* when you tend to agree with the writer.

QD

chapter 3

COMMON ERRORS

This is just the sort of nonsense up with which I will not put.
    ~Winston Churchill

Winston Churchill, England's prime minister during World War II, was famous for his wit and his eloquence. I doubt he ever made many "mistakes" in language, but his concern for what grammarians call "correctness" didn't stop him from making fun of the sometimes absurd rules that grammarians create. In the quote above, he's cleverly ridiculing one of those rules, namely not to end a sentence with a preposition (*up*, in this case). Grammatical rules are intended to enhance clarity, but Churchill's sentence illustrates that blindly adhering to (some) grammatical rules can produce comical and ridiculous sentences.

Correctness is a complicated subject, one that we English teachers don't always agree on. And the rules change over time as people refuse to conform to them; a hundred or so years ago, for example, this was considered correct: "He forgat his book."

A more contemporary example: people have started to use the word *anxious* to mean *excited*, as in, *I am anxious to see the new restaurant.* But the word's traditional meaning has to do with worry and anxiety, not excited anticipation: *I am anxious about my test results.* Still, many people are unaware of the "real" meaning of the word and use it to convey excitement. Can we really say it's wrong if so many people use it that way? Eventually, the dictionary will most likely offer both definitions, to reflect how people are actually using the word.

In short, the "rules" are always in flux. But that doesn't change the fact that you should learn and follow them in your writing, particularly in academic and professional situations.

COMMONLY CONFUSED WORDS

3.1   accept / except

Please **accept** my gift of $14,000 so you can buy a car.

Any car is fine, **except** a yellow one.

3.2   all right   not *alright*

The man left the emergency room when he decided he felt **all right**.

This usage is informal, so you shouldn't use it in academic writing.

3.3   a lot   not *alot*

A lot of people went to see the artist's video of David Beckham sleeping.

In academic writing, it would be better to express a large number more precisely: More than 2,000 visitors saw the artist's video in the exhibition's first week.

3.4   a part / apart

As two words, it means that he *belongs* to the club:

He is **a part** of the oldest club on campus.

As one word, it means that this one expense is *separate from* the others.

Apart from her car insurance, she paid all her bills without her parents' help.

3.5   effect / affect

Effect is (almost always) a noun:

Moving out of his parents' house had at least one positive **effect**: It forced him to get a job.

Affect is (almost always) a verb:

Moving out of his parents' house negatively **affected** his bank statement.

A complication you will only rarely encounter: *Effect* can also be a verb. In that case, it means *to bring about,* or *to cause to occur.*

The Board of Education hopes to **effect** change on a system-wide basis.

An additional complication you will encounter even less often: *Affect* can also be a noun, meaning emotional state; the pronunciation is different too, with the stress on the first syllable.

The referee's pleasant **affect** prevented the players from yelling at him, even when he made a bad call.

3.6   imply / infer

Speakers and writers *imply* things:

The speaker **implied** that college freshmen were irresponsible.

Listeners and readers *infer*—or come to a conclusion about something—based on what they hear and read.

We **inferred** from the speaker's comments that he believed college freshmen to be irresponsible.

3.7   it's / its   not *its'*

It's is a contraction (the apostrophe indicates that a letter has been "contracted," or taken away) and always means one of two things: *It is* or *It has.*

> **It's** been raining all day. (It has been raining all day.)

> **It's** going to be a long day. (It is going to be a long day.)

Its is always possessive:

> The dog wagged **its** tail.

(If you wrote *it's* by accident, the sentence would say: The dog wagged it is tail.) See pages 46–48 for possession rules.

3.8   less / fewer

Less is for amounts that can't be counted; *fewer* is for things that can be.

> Ted has **less** hair than Greg.

> Ironically, though, Ted owns **fewer** wigs than Greg.

And yes, this means that when you see a sign in a grocery store saying "10 items or less," it really should say "10 items or fewer."

3.9   lose / loose

Lose is a verb; *loose* is an adjective:

> If you keep playing like that, you're going to **lose** the game.

> When the bolts came **loose**, the wheel spun off the axle.

3.10   then / than

Then shows when something happened:

> We ate breakfast, and **then** we went hiking.

Than makes a comparison:

> Stewie's argument was more persuasive **than** Brian's.

3.11   there /their / they're

There shows location:

> He put the clothes over **there**.

Their shows possession ("ownership"):

> That is **their** house.

They're is a contraction of *they are*:

> **They're** not going to be home. (They are not going to be home.)

3.12   to / too

To is a preposition and an "infinitive":

> I'm going **to** the game. He's planning **to** quit.

Too is an "intensifier":

> He has **too** much rice. I was **too** tired to go.

3.13   who / which / that

Don't use *that* when you refer to people.

> **NO** Those are the students **that** wrote the editorial.

> **YES** Those are the students **who** wrote the editorial.

Use *that* when you refer to inanimate objects:

> Here are the papers **that** need to be revised.

Note: you can also use *which*, but most American grammarians recommend *that*. In the next sentence, however, *which* is the only correct choice:

> The revised papers, **which** I've attached to this e-mail, are ready for your comments.

A simple guideline: If you have a construction like this and you're trying to decide between *that* and *which*, use *that* if there's no comma, and *which* if there is. See also pages 49-50 or do an Internet search for restrictive versus nonrestrictive clauses.

3.14   who's / whose

Who's is a contraction of Who is.

> **Who's** the man with the crooked hat? (Who is the man with the crooked hat?)

Whose is possessive; it shows that something belongs to someone or something.

> That's the man **whose** hat is crooked.

3.15   would have / would've   not *would of*

Writers make this mistake for a good reason—because they write what they hear, or what they say.

> His argument **would have** been more persuasive if he had included better evidence.

Note: In formal writing, it's best to avoid contractions like *would've*.

3.16   you and I vs. you and me (and related errors)

Whenever you hear "That's between she and I," the speaker has made a grammatical mistake, one that you should learn how to avoid in your writing.

Grammar people call it an example of "hyper-correction," meaning that when we say something like "between she and I," it's because we believe we're being extra conscientious, grammatically speaking. We remember being corrected by English teachers when we said things like, "Me and Josh are going to the movie." The teacher would have said, sternly, "You mean, *Josh and I* are going to the movie."

And the teacher would be right because *Josh and I* are a subject (they're doing something), not an object (having something done to them, or receiving an action). So if you said, "The teacher hates Josh and me," you'd be correct, because in that case *Josh and me* are objects—they are receiving the teacher's hatred (or what they imagine to be her hatred; she was probably just trying to help).

Let's look at some examples.

Subject   Object

Sally loves Hank.

When you introduce another person being loved, that's when things get complicated—both in love and grammar. I should say, it gets complicated when the other person is a pronoun: **I / me** instead of Fred, **she / her** instead of Wanda, etc.

Sally loves Hank and **(I or me?)**.

The trick is to mentally remove *Hank and*; then it's easy to see the right choice. Think of it this way: You'd never be tempted to say, *Sally loves I*, right? So why would you be tempted to say, *Sally loves Hank and I*?

YES   Sally loves Hank and **me**.

Now let's change Hank to a pronoun too. Is it *he* or *him*? Same principle: You wouldn't say, *Sally loves he*. You'd say, *Sally loves him*. So:

YES   Sally loves both **him and me**.

Believe it or not, that's correct. It should *not* be, *Sally loves both he and I.* Never ever ever. No matter how many times you hear people on TV say it—it's not right, and educated people know the difference.

Note: If you're bothered by how your sentence sounds when you write it correctly, consider changing things around. Instead of saying, Oliver sent an invitation to Betsy and me (*not* Betsy and I), you could reverse the order: *When Betsy and I received Oliver's invitation, we hoped we would be out of town that weekend.*

When you use a preposition (*between* in this example), the same rules apply:

> **NO** That is between he and I.

> **YES** That is between him and me.

THE IMPORTANCE OF SOUND

Sound does matter in language, both in writing and speaking; when the grammatically correct way of writing something results in a sentence that sounds wrong, try to rewrite it. Often this means changing the entire sentence rather than just a word or two.

3.17   your / you're

Your shows possession:

> **Your** hat is crooked. **Your** beliefs are ridiculous.

The second example is abstract. See Abstract Possession on page 48.

You're is a contraction of you are:

> **You're** going to be late. (You are going to be late.)

COMMON SENTENCE ERRORS

Think of your paper as if it were a house. You, the writer, are like the architect who designs the house. (You're also the general contractor, the electrician, the painter, etc., but we'll keep the analogy simple for now.) When it comes to grammar, though, you're more like an engineer than an architect.

Engineers are the ones who decide if a house is going to work, structurally. When the architect designs a balcony that hangs thirty feet over the back wall of the house, it's the engineer who would say, "That will collapse and kill someone." The engineer is less concerned with how the house is going to look, and much more concerned with whether or not the it's going to stand up and keep everyone inside dry.

We're not talking about what would look interesting. We're talking about whether or not the thing "works" grammatically—because if you have a paper full of flawed sentences, it's like a house where the walls are in the wrong places, or built from the wrong materials. It might look like a house, but it won't be safe. Now apply that analogy to a paper with numerous sentence errors: It might look like a paper, but it won't really make a lot of sense, and it might even fail in its most basic mission—to communicate with a reader.

3.18   RUN-ON / COMMA SPLICE

A run-on sentence has more than one complete thought in it; it becomes a run-on when you don't connect—or separate—those thoughts grammatically.

> Jim drove his car into a pile of snow he could not get the car back onto the road.

In that "sentence," there are two complete thoughts; the first one ends after the word *snow*. That's a pretty obvious error, and not one that many students would make. But this version of the same mistake is less obvious:

> Jim drove his car into a pile of snow **then** he could not get the car back onto the road.

This sounds better, but it's still a run-on, because **then** doesn't have the grammatical power to connect the two complete thoughts.

Note: A comma splice has essentially the same problem as a run-on, but it has a comma between the two complete thoughts—which still isn't enough to connect the parts:

> Jim drove his car into a pile of snow, he could not get the car back onto the road.

Run-ons and comma splices can be corrected in two basic ways—either by separating the complete thoughts (with a period or semicolon), or by connecting them (with a variety of methods).

Separating with a period—acceptable but often simplistic

Jim drove his car into a pile of snow. He could not get the car back onto the road.

Connecting —a better solution

With a coordinating conjunction (comma *before* the conjunction):

Jim drove his car into a pile of snow, **and** he could not get the car back onto the road.

With a "dependent word" (see below for a list of these):

After Jim drove his car into a pile of snow, he could not get the car back onto the road.

Or with a dependent word, reversing the parts (and changing a pronoun):

Jim could not get his car back onto the road **after** he drove it into a pile of snow.

Common Dependent Words		
because	though	while
when	unless	after
even though	until	as
although if	whatever	as if
in order to	whenever	before
since	whether	even if

Connecting with a semi-colon (;)

A semi-colon functions almost exactly like a period, at least grammatically. It has the power to connect two complete thoughts, just like a period.

Jim drove his car into a pile of snow; he could not get the car back onto the road.

This isn't a great place to use a semi-colon, though. It's just as simplistic as using the period, and there's no good reason to use a semi-colon here. Generally, I'd suggest avoiding semi-colons, though they can be useful when you have a long sentence where the ideas are closely connected.

If you do want to use a semi-colon, it's often a good idea to use a "conjunctive adverb" like *however* or *therefore* immediately after it. (See below for full list.) The conjunctive adverb also functions as a transition within your sentence, so this can help the reader understand the connection between the two parts of the sentence more easily.

Be careful with these; used incorrectly, they often lead to run-ons or comma splices. Conjunctive adverbs typically need to be used after a period or a semicolon and are always followed by a comma:

NO The car was completely stuck, however it did not appear to be damaged.

YES The car was completely stuck; however, it did not appear to be damaged.

Conjunctive Adverbs

however	consequently	nonetheless
therefore	conversely	otherwise
indeed	finally	similarly
moreover	furthermore	still
subsequently	likewise	then
accordingly	meanwhile	thus

3.19   FRAGMENT

A fragment is an incomplete sentence. It can happen for a variety of reasons, most often because you've made one part of the sentence dependent—without giving it another part that's independent to balance it. Here's an example:

When there is no more gas left and cheaper sources of fuel can't be found.

It's that first word, "when," that makes the sentence a fragment—because it's a dependent word in this case. Like most fragments, the sentence leaves the reader hanging, waiting for something else. What you're waiting for is the independent clause, the thing that will make the sentence complete:

> When there is no more gas left and cheaper sources of fuel can't be found, more research will be devoted to alternative energies.

Fragments *can* be good

Fragments aren't always a mistake. Experienced writers use them for good effect—they can break up the rhythm of your sentences and provide emphasis, as in this example:

> Storing explicit memories and, equally important, forming connections between them requires strong mental concentration, amplified by repetition or by intense intellectual or emotional engagement. The sharper the attention, the sharper the memory. (193)
>
> ~ Nicholas Carr, *The Shallows: What the Internet Is Doing to Our Brains*

The second sentence is the fragment, of course (there's no verb). But it's effective here because the sentence that precedes it is long and complex. The simplicity of the second sentence provides a quick, accessible way of thinking about the complex information in the previous sentence.

Purposeful fragments can help balance long sentences and provide a quick punch of information. But use them sparingly—too many fragmented sentences (even when written intentionally) will look gimmicky, and they will lose the power to grab the reader's attention.

3.20   SUBJECT-VERB AGREEMENT

Subjects and verbs have to agree "in number":

> **NO** The paper **go** into that drawer.

> **YES** The paper **goes** into that drawer.

3.21   COMPOUND SUBJECT (SUBJECT-VERB AGREEMENT)

When you have a two-part subject joined by *and*, you need a plural verb:

The chair and the table **are** in the truck.

Some writers are thrown off by the fact that table (which is singular) is right next to the verb, which might make them choose *is* for the verb instead of *are*. But *are* is correct because chair and table, together, become plural.

When you have a two-part subject joined by *or*, you choose the verb based on the subject closest to the verb.

Singular

The plumber or his assistant **does** a final inspection of the work.

Plural

The plumber or his assistants **do** a final inspection of the work.

3.22   THERE IS / THERE ARE (SUBJECT-VERB-AGREEMENT)

When you start a sentence with one of these constructions, you have to choose the right verb (*is* or *are*) based on whether the subject is singular or plural.

There **is** one way to get rid of fleas on your dog.

There **are** many ways your dog can get fleas.

In the first sentence, the subject is *way*, which is singular.

In the second sentence, the subject is *ways*, which is plural.

Note: Starting a sentence with *There is* or *There are* is weak—try to rewrite your sentence to avoid this construction. (See Chapter 6: Editing & Proofreading, especially page 88.)

3.23 -ING SUBJECT (SUBJECT-VERB AGREEMENT)

When your subject is an –ing word (also called a gerund), you need a singular verb. (This error, by the way, appeared in the *New York Times*.)

Singular   Plural

NO The awarding of contracts to Pearson in Iowa and Utah **illustrate** the problem.

Singular   Singular

YES The awarding of contracts to Pearson in Iowa and Utah **illustrates** the problem.

3.24 PRONOUN REFERENCE "ERRORS"

This is an exciting moment. I've written five editions of this book over 15 years, and up until today, February 27, 2020, I have always considered the sample sentence you see below (with the ? next to it) to be an error. So why is this exciting? Because language has changed.

Yes, this is happening all the time, as I mentioned at the beginning of this chapter. But it's rare to watch a grammatical rule simply stop being a rule—within a matter of about one year. Anyway, the rule used to say that the following sentence was grammatical incorrect:

Singular   Plural

? **Each student** must submit **their** financial aid form by Friday at 5 p.m.

Grammar people didn't like that sentence because, they reasoned, *each* means one and *they* means more than one—so the two parts didn't match up.

Recently, though, two important organizations (*Merriam-Webster Dictionary* and the American Psychological Association) both ruled that *their* is perfectly acceptable in the sentence above. After consulting with my colleagues, I'm ready to move forward and declare that sentence grammatically correct. Hoorah for language change! So:

YES **Each student** must submit **their** financial aid form by Friday at 5 p.m.

Now, having said that, you should be aware that some traditionalists will still object to that construction. And in some cases, you might want to switch to a plural subject anyway, which means that you could re-write it this way:

YES **Students** must submit **their** financial aid forms by Friday at 5 p.m.

By the way, this used to be considered correct but is now generally regarded as clumsy:

NO Each student must submit his or her financial aid form by Friday at 5 p.m.

Note: A separate but related issue is that some people now identify as "gender non-binary," meaning they do not see themselves as stricly male or female. In other words, a person may appear female but not want to be identified as *she* or *her*. The person may ask to be referred to with the pronouns *they, them,* and *their.* Like this: I saw Sheila recently, and *they* had just started a new job.

This sounds unusual to strict grammarians, but most people (even strict grammarians) would agree that it's important to honor a request not to attach a gendered pronoun to someone when *they* have made it clear they object. In just the last few years, a number of "style guides" have approved of this "non-standard" pronoun usage, including the MLA, the *Chicago Manual of Style,* the *Associated Press Stylebook* (the standard for most newspapers), the *New York Times,* and the APA (see Chapter 9).

3.25   FAULTY PARALLELISM

Parallelism means that two or more elements are consistent with each other.

Parallel   Not parallel

NO   The college's student government is responsible for recruiting new members, submitting a budget, and **enforcement of all policies.**

Not parallel

The first two responsibilities are parallel to each other, because they both begin with an -ing verb and then follow with a noun. The third responsibility, in order to be parallel, must also start with an -ing verb (enforcing) and follow with a noun.

 The college's student government is responsible for recruiting new members, submitting a budget, and **enforcing all policies.**

Parallel

A FEW RULES WORTH LEARNING

I've always believed that English teachers rely too much on rules—and that students learn to write more clearly as a result of reading and practice. Still, you'll avoid a lot of mistakes if you refer to these guidelines for apostrophes, commas, titles, and capitalization.

3.26   APOSTROPHES FOR CONTRACTIONS

A contraction means that something becomes smaller. With words, contractions are formed with apostrophes: is not = isn't.

The apostrophe here shows that a letter has been removed. The principle is the same even if the apostrophe replaces more letters:

would have = would've

Note: Avoid contractions in formal academic writing.

3.27   APOSTROPHES FOR POSSESSION

When we speak, we create the "sound" of possession by adding an *ess* sound. But when we write, we use an apostrophe.

I offer four rules for apostrophes here. If you learn the first two, you'll get the apostrophe right 70 percent of the time. Learn all four and you'll never make an apostrophe mistake.

#1: WHEN *NOT* TO USE AN APOSTROPHE

Don't add apostrophes to words that are simply plurals. In this example, some people would be tempted to put an apostrophe somewhere in the word *cars*.

> Five cars were left in the parking lot overnight.

But nothing "belongs" to the cars here, so there's no apostrophe.

#2: ADD 'S TO THE END OF THE WORD

In most cases, just add **'s** to the word doing the possessing. Here, the trunk "belongs to"—or is a part of—the car, so you add **'s** to car.

> One car's trunk had been broken into.

Here, one cat "possesses" a paw:

> The cat's paw got caught in the door.

The rule is the same if the person/animal/thing doing the possessing ends with the letter s; pretend that the cat is named James:

> James's paw got caught in the door.

Also, it doesn't matter if the cat had managed to get two paws stuck in the door—the possession rule would be the same:

> The cat's paws got caught in the door.

Okay, it probably matters to the cat, but it doesn't matter to us, at least not in terms of getting the apostrophe right.

#3: ADD S' TO THE END OF SOME WORDS

When more than one person or thing is doing the possessing, the apostrophe usually goes after the **s**. In this example, *cars* is plural in the first sentence (so no apostrophe), but possessive in the second sentence (so it needs an apostrophe).

> Five cars were left in the parking lot overnight. All the cars' windshields were smashed.

Also remember that it wouldn't matter if we added an adjective, i.e., the cars' *dirty* windshields.

#4: SOME COMPLICATIONS

The plural form of most words ends with an s: tables, chairs, elephants, houses, trees, and so on. But some words—like *women, people, men*—form a plural without the final s. When the plural form of a word does not end in s, add 's.

> The women's room is down the hall, on your left.

(The room that "belongs to" women is down the hall.)

NOT A RULE, BUT SOMETHING TO BE AWARE OF: ABSTRACT POSSESSION

Often, the idea of possession is obvious: Something "belongs" to someone: Jim's hat, or Tina's car. But there's another form of "possession" that is less obvious, mainly because it isn't physical. Think of it as abstract, or conceptual, possession. For example:

> Mike's anger caused him to lose his job.

Does Mike "possess" his anger? Not in any physical sense—but in a grammatical sense, yes. The most common form of abstract possession is emotional: Mike's anger, Tina's love of her children, Paul's fear of dogs, etc. But other types of possession are even harder to detect because they involve what I'll call an "abstract state of being."

> Mike's inability to control his anger caused him to lose his job.

Again, it's hard to think of "inability" as belonging to Mike, but it does.

3.28 COMMAS

Six rules cover just about every use of the comma. Here they are:

AFTER INTRODUCTORY MATERIAL

After the judge's recess, the plaintiff disappeared.

Nonetheless, all the cars were ticketed.

AROUND AN "INTERRUPTION"

James, the oldest boy in the class, was also the tallest.

WITH ITEMS IN A LIST OR SERIES

The recipe calls for apples, pears, peaches, and cinnamon.

Note: The comma after the next-to-last item in the list—*peaches*, in this case—is the subject of great controversy among grammar geeks. Some consider it optional, while others insist it must be included. If you're curious, Google *Oxford comma*.

BETWEEN TWO COMPLETE THOUGHTS, WITH A CONJUNCTION

The protesters made a lot of noise, but most people ignored them.

WITH MANY USES OF *WHICH* (AKA NONRESTRICTIVE CLAUSES)

Her favorite food was artichokes, which he found repulsive.

I explain the grammatical rule in the next few examples, but it may be just as helpful for you to simply listen for the slight pause that usually occurs in these constructions.

When to use *that* versus *which* can be confusing, particularly when you're trying to determine whether or not you need a comma; grammatically, the key is to know whether you're dealing with a restrictive or a nonrestrictive clause. Restrictive clauses generally don't have a comma:

Cell phones that ring during movies are extremely annoying.

Here, the meaning of cell phones is *restricted*—the sentence says that in *one specific circumstance* (during a movie) cell phones are annoying. No comma is needed.

But a sentence with a non-restrictive clause does need a comma (or two):

Cell phones, which became widely available in the mid-90s, can be extremely useful.

Here, the meaning is *not* restricted—the sentence says that cell phones can be extremely useful. The other piece of information is not essential to the meaning of the sentence. (Yes, this example is very similar to the "interruption" rule.)

WITH QUOTATIONS (SEE ALSO CHAPTER 4)

Red Barber once said, "Baseball is dull only to dull minds."

Note: If the quote flows grammatically within the sentence, then the comma is usually omitted:

Red Barber once described baseball as being dull "only to dull minds."

3.29   TITLES OF SOURCES

Generally, titles of shorter works go inside quotation marks; titles of longer works are italicized.

QUOTATION MARKS

Articles, essays, poems, short story titles, song titles, TV episodes, etc.

News article: "A Guide to Smartphone Manners"

Essay: "Hidden Intellectualism"

Short story: "Boys and Girls"

Poem: "The Red Wheelbarrow"

| Episode of a TV show: | "The Red Wedding"
(episode of *Game of Thrones*) |
| Song: | "Soliloquy of Chaos"
(from the album *Daily Operation*) |

ITALICS

Book:	*Moby-Dick*
Textbook:	*Quick and Dirty: A Compact Guide to Writing, Reading, and Research*
Album:	*In the Aeroplane Over the Sea*
Movie:	*Lost in Translation*
Television show:	*BoJack Horseman*

3.30   THE TITLE OF *YOUR* PAPER

Generally, you capitalize all the "important" words. Always capitalize the first word and the last word of your title; also capitalize the first word after a colon (if you use one, as you should—see page 84). Also, these are the rules for MLA formatting; APA is slightly different (see page 180).

Don't capitalize the following:

articles: a, an, the

prepositions (even long ones): of, on, to, for, with, about, through, between, among, around (and many others)

conjunctions: and, but, or, so, yet, nor, for

infinitive: to

Example:

An Analysis of Symbiotic Relationships among Birds, Bees, and Flies

Note that *among* is not capitalized because it's a preposition.

Also, when you put a title on your own paper, don't do anything to it—no quotation marks, no italics, no bold. Nothing. The only exception to this is if you have a quote within your title, like this:

Landscape, Memory, and Myth in Heaney's "Personal Helicon"

3.31   CAPITALIZATION

PEOPLE'S NAMES

Ernest Hemingway, Homer J. Simpson

PLACES

Paris, France; Wheeling, West Virginia; North Carolina's Outer Banks

Complication: Some "places" don't get capitalized: southern Virginia (because there is no place by that name), western Massachusetts

However, you do capitalize regions in some cases (but not compass directions):

Many people died when the West was settled. (Region.)

Chicopee is west of Worcester. (Compass direction.)

LANGUAGES / PEOPLE / CUISINES

English, French, Chinese, Russian, Portuguese, etc.

ORGANIZATIONS / INSTITUTIONS

Congress, the Department of Labor, Seattle Central Community College, United Auto Workers (because it's the formal name of a union)

BRAND NAMES

Kleenex, Apple (the computer), Panasonic, Tide (laundry detergent)

PROFESSIONAL TITLES / ACADEMIC TITLES

Typically, if someone's title comes before his or her name, you capitalize it; if it comes after, you don't:

I met with Vice President Bausch for almost an hour last week.

The meeting was led by Robert Bausch, vice president of the college.

ADDITIONAL RESOURCES

To learn more about grammar and usage, I recommend the Khan Academy site—an Internet search for *Khan Academy grammar* will get you there. You can watch video tutorials and take quizzes to improve your understanding of the concepts in this chapter. I also recommend the site at Purdue University; a search for *owl purdue grammar* should take you to the right place. It's not as interactive as the Khan site, but the information there is excellent.

chapter 4

WRITING WITH SOURCES

I am disillusioned enough to know that no man's opinion on any subject is worth a damn unless backed up with enough genuine information to make him really know what he's talking about.
~ H. P. Lovecraft

Most writing that you do in college will involve not just *your* ideas, opinions, and observations—but also the ideas, opinions, and research of *others*. This chapter is designed to help you learn how to *interact* with your sources. I emphasize that word because it's important for you to use your sources in a purposeful way. It's not good enough simply to dump six or eight quotations from a couple of articles into your paper—you need to introduce them, provide context for them, comment on them, and compare them to other sources.

An academic paper is a kind of conversation: When you interact with your sources, you're in conversation with them. It becomes more complex when you have multiple sources—in the same way that it becomes more challenging to have a face-to-face conversation when multiple people are trying to speak.

First, we'll focus on how you incorporate ideas and information from your sources. For most of these examples, I'll be using a book by Michael Pollan as the source; the book is *The Omnivore's Dilemma*, about food and agriculture in America.

"HERE'S WHAT SOMEONE ELSE HAS TO SAY."

When you use source material, it's important that you do so responsibly, which means *summarizing*, *paraphrasing*, or *quoting* accurately. Typically, you want to use a signal phrase (such as "According to Michael Pollan…") to introduce the source material; this will make it clear that the idea or information belongs to a source, not to you.

Summarize: to state the main idea of a text (or part of a text) in a shortened form.

> Note: A summary is only a fraction of the length of the original; you can summarize a three-page essay in a few sentences, but you can't summarize it in three pages—the summary must be a small fraction of the total. For a longer work, like a 300-page novel, you can summarize it in a few sentences or a few paragraphs, depending on how much detail you want to go into.

Paraphrase: to put someone else's idea into your own words.

Quote: to use the exact words of your source.

"HERE'S WHAT I HAVE TO SAY ABOUT THAT."

This is where *you* enter the conversation, and essentially you have three options, with some overlap:

- to use the source in **support** of something you're saying
- to **disagree** with an assertion from a source
- to **extend** or build upon an idea from a source

It should always be clear to your reader *why* you're using source material—it should be in service of an idea you're developing in your paper.

HOW MUCH SOURCE MATERIAL SHOULD YOUR PAPER HAVE?

The answer to this question depends on a number of factors—the discipline (psychology, linguistics, art history, biology, etc.) you're working in, the type of paper you're writing, your professor's expectations, and so on.

For most research papers, roughly 20 to 50 percent of the paper should come from sources. The other 50 to 80 percent should be you interpreting the evidence and directing our thinking.

PRIMARY VS. SECONDARY SOURCES

Many professors will require that you do both primary (meaning first or original) and secondary research. In the excerpt you're about to read, from Pollan's book, his research on prices of particular items at a grocery store is *primary* research. Most likely, he took notes in a grocery store and/or examined advertising from stores. He didn't rely on some other researcher for this information—he examined the "data" himself. If, however, you use Pollan's book as a source, then his book and everything in it would be a *secondary* source for you.

Primary sources are often pure data (a government census, enrollment figures at a college, city tax records), but they can also be documents created or recorded by "participants" in an event: letters and diaries written by Civil War soldiers, for example, or video of the 9/11 terrorist attacks.

Secondary sources, on the other hand, are those that interpret, comment on, analyze, or make arguments about those events: a book that argues how Confederate soldiers became increasingly hopeless as the war progressed, or an essay proposing a new theory about terrorist cells in the U.S.

Almost all of your verbs should be in present tense, as the **VERBS** examples in this chapter show: *Pollan asserts*, not *Pollan asserted*. A couple of exceptions: If you're discussing a historical event, like World War II, then you use the past tense. Be aware that the rules are different for APA-formatted papers (see page 163). Also, choose good verbs, like these, all of which are better than *says* or *states*:

| asserts | claims | argues | suggests | observes | maintains |

SUMMARIZING, PARAPHRASING, AND QUOTING

These three skills are essential in academic writing. I'll cover each one separately, and to illustrate I'll use an excerpt from page 136 of Pollan's book. In this chapter, Pollan is dicussing how organic food has become a big industry, and in this paragraph he's focused on how pricing works in traditional supermarkets.

Wordy labels, point-of-purchase brochures, and certification schemes are supposed to make an obscure and complicated food chain more legible to the consumer. In the industrial food economy, virtually the only information that travels along the food chain linking producer and consumer is price. Just look at the typical newspaper ad for a supermarket. The sole quality on display here is actually a quantity: tomatoes $0.69 a pound; ground chuck $1.09 a pound; eggs $0.99 a dozen—special this week. Is there any other category of product sold on such a reductive basis? The bare-bones information travels in both directions, of course, and farmers who get the message that consumers care only about price will themselves care only about yield. This is how a cheap food economy reinforces itself.

SUMMARIZING

The goal of summarizing is to capture the main idea of the source material—whether it's a paragraph, a chapter, or an entire book—as accurately as possible. Remember that your summary must be shorter than what you're summarizing. In this example, I've reduced seven sentences to one:

SIGNAL PHRASE

Pollan asserts that the industrial food economy continues to dominate because neither farmers nor traditional grocery stores are motivated to provide any information beyond price to consumers (136).

You might find it reassuring to know that it took me—the supposed expert in these matters—about five minutes to write that one sentence. I had to keep thinking about which information to include and how the ideas related to each other. I wrote it three different ways before I was satisfied with it.

In a typical research paper, you might use four or five (or many more) sources. Every time you move from one source to another, it's a moment

THE IMPORTANCE OF **SIGNAL PHRASES**

of potential confusion for the reader, particularly when you're also making your own assertions. When you use signal phrases consistently, it helps the reader keep track of who's saying what.

PARAPHRASING

To paraphrase is to put a writer's idea in your own words. Most students go about this in the most counter-productive way: they stare at the original sentence and try to think of synonyms for the key words, then put together a "new" sentence that has different words but often sounds awkward. Instead, the best way to paraphrase is this:

1. Read the sentence(s) closely and be sure that you understand everything the writer is saying. Pay particular attention to how ideas relate to each other, especially when the writer is showing causality (one thing causing another).

2. Close the book, or the web page, or whatever it is you're reading. Reconstruct the idea in your head in language that makes sense to you. If you're not looking at the original, you'll be less inclined to repeat its wording or structure, and the sentence you write will sound more natural.

3. Start writing, still without looking at the original. Don't worry if you repeat a word or two that appeared in the original.

4. Compare your version to the original. The idea from the original should be intact, but the paraphrase should sound like *your* writing. If necessary, think of synonyms to replace key words you repeat from the original.

Here's an example where I paraphrase one of Pollan's sentences. His sentence:

> The bare-bones information travels in both directions, of course, and farmers who get the message that consumers care only about price will themselves care only about yield.

First, I made sure I understood the idea—that farmers have changed their practices because (causality) they know what motivates consumers.

This is what I came up with. I believe that Pollan's ideas are intact, as is the relationship between them, i.e., the cause and effect. And I believe that the voice is mine, not Pollan's.

SIGNAL PHRASE

Pollan asserts that because many farmers believe consumers are only concerned with cost, the farmers then focus only on how much of any particular crop they can produce (136).

Here's another version, without a signal phrase:

> Farmers who know that consumers are concerned with cost alone will in turn focus only on how much of any particular crop they can produce (Pollan 136).

SLOPPY PARAPHRASE = PLAGIARISM

First, be sure that you cite your source properly. Yes, even if you put source material into your own words, you still must give credit to your sources for their ideas. If you don't, it's plagiarism. (See page 64 for more on plagiarism.)

Second, be aware that if you follow the sentence structure or language of the original too closely, this may be considered *inappropriate borrowing* and thus also a form of plagiarism. For example, the following paraphrase of the Pollan sentence would be deemed unacceptable by most professors:

> Pollan asserts that the basic information moves both ways, so farmers who learn that grocery store customers only care about how much things cost will themselves care only about how much they can produce (136).

Why is this unacceptable? Because it follows the wording of the original too closely. Even though it's properly documented, the language and sentence structure are too similar to Pollan's.

QUOTING

Once you've decided to quote rather than paraphrase, you have one more decision to make: Do you want to quote an entire sentence (or more), or only part of a sentence?

QUOTING AN ENTIRE SENTENCE

This is the easiest way to quote because there are no complicated rules about punctuation. I'll choose a sentence that fits my first reason for quoting (see page 61), the one that says to quote a writer when they say something in a particularly interesting way:

> SIGNAL PHRASE
>
> As Michael Pollan observes, "The bare-bones information travels in both directions, of course, and farmers who get the message that consumers care only about price will themselves care only about yield" (136).

It looks simple, but many students make mistakes with this kind of quotation. It's essential that you have some kind of introduction for the quotation. You should never have a sentence that's only a quotation without any kind of context. The "context" I've provided, *As Michael Pollan observes*, is minimal; sometimes you'll want to do more, but generally this is adequate.

Another way to quote an entire sentence from a source is to use a colon. This will typically mean that you have a longer signal phrase, one that contains more information than just who the source is. In this example, imagine that the previous couple of sentences have been discussing how different types of food are treated in terms of government subsidies:

> Pollan makes the contrast between junk food ingredients and *real* food even more pointed: "We subsidize high-fructose corn syrup in this country, but not carrots" (108).

Here, the quotation functions as the evidence for what I've written before the colon.

QUOTING PART OF A SENTENCE

This is often more effective than quoting an entire sentence. It allows you to partially paraphrase a writer's idea but still show his or her exact wording, briefly. Quoting part of a sentence is useful when a writer says something memorable or interesting—or simply difficult to paraphrase—in just a word or phrase. Here I quote part of Pollan's first sentence:

> Pollan claims that stores like Whole Foods use these techniques to "make an obscure and complicated food chain more legible to the consumer" (136).

The key to making the partial quotation work is to make the quoted material flows grammatically within the entire sentence. If you took the quotation marks away, the sentence would still make sense grammatically—it would still sound like a good sentence. (Though, of course, you wouldn't want to actually do this because that would be plagiarism.)

You can also quote a single word, which puts great emphasis on that word:

> Pollan describes the contemporary agricultural economy as "industrial" (136).

When I was writing that sentence, I had the feeling that I wanted to explore this idea further—something about calling attention to that single word *industrial* made me think that the next sentence should extend Pollan's thinking. This is where I'm beginning to "enter the conversation":

> Pollan describes the contemporary agricultural process as "industrial" (136); this makes plain the connections between farming and big business and reveals their shared qualities. Both are primarily concerned with profits and often less concerned with sustainability.

Note that I put the in-text citation immediately after that word, which helps the reader understand that what comes next is *my* thinking.

Reminder: This is just a quick overview of the key things you need to know about quoting. In Chapters 8 and 9, I cover additional guidelines that you're likely to need: how to use ellipses (the three dots) and brackets (for words that you change in a quotation), and how to quote someone who's being quoted.

HOW DO YOU DECIDE WHETHER TO QUOTE OR PARAPHRASE?

Your first instinct should be to paraphrase. Which is not to say that you shouldn't quote your sources—quotations are essential, and they can help you be more efficient and accurate. The danger is that when you quote too much, your paper may sound more like a jumble of other writers than you.

Here are three good reasons to quote rather than paraphrase:

1. Your source says something in a particularly compelling or interesting way. If the specific language the source uses is important to our understanding of the idea, you should quote that language.

2. Your source says something that is similar to, or supportive of, a point you're making. In this case, the exact words of the source can help back up a claim you're making.

3. Your source says something that you disagree with, and part of your analysis focuses on shades of meaning that can be seen in the precise word choice.

INTERACTING WITH SOURCES

Up to now, this chapter has been concerned with how you represent sources in your writing; earlier in the chapter, I referred to it as "Here's what someone else has to say."

Now we come to the next part: "Here's what I have to say about that."

The first part is important, of course—because if you don't present your source material correctly, you could be plagiarizing. But the second part is equally important because it's in your interaction with sources that your reader learns *why* you're telling us what someone else has said, and how it relates to your paper's overall purpose.

Interaction is a three-step process:

1. **Write a sentence that prepares the reader for the source material.**

2. **Present the source material via quotation, paraphrase, or summary.**

3. **Explain or comment on the source material.**

Here are the three steps in action (taken from sample paper on page 187):

> **1** For many professors, though, the key issue is not whether individual students are giving the professor their full attention; instead, they are concerned that one student's use of a device can be distracting to *other* students. **2** Sana et al. reported that students "in view of multitasking peers scored significantly lower on the test than [those] not in view of multitasking peers" (29). **3** In other words, students did worse on tests when they could see another student who was distracted.

1 This sentence starts by making a transition from the previous paragraph, then provides context for the research that comes next.

2 Here's the source material, which gives evidence for the idea in the previous sentence.

3 The next sentence explains the source material.

The next example is more sophisticated because it does more than simply restate the source material (it's from the sample paper, page 184):

> **1** In order to understand recent research that examines the effect of laptops on note-taking and learning, it is useful to understand what happens when people take notes. **2a.** In the early 1970s, Francis Di Vesta and Susan Gray found that the connection between note-taking and learning had two components, "encoding" and "external storage" (qtd. in Mueller and Oppenheimer). **2b.** Encoding is what happens while the person is taking notes, when the brain is processing what the note-taker hears and sees. External storage is what happens when the person tries to recall the information later, as for example on an exam. **3** The distinction is important because it could reveal more about the differences between taking notes by hand versus on a laptop.

1   The first sentence sets up why the source material will be important.

2a.   The first part of the source material combines paraphrase and quotation.

2b.   The next two sentences use paraphrase to explain the terminology of the research.

3   The final sentence explains the significance of the research for *this* paper. (This is the final sentence of that particular paragraph, and the next paragraph explores the importance of the distinction more specifically.)

Earlier in this chapter, I put a lot of emphasis on the importance of learning **SUMMARY ≠ ANALYSIS** how to summarize your sources. Bear in mind, though, that summary is only useful in your paper when you put it to some use. The example above begins the process of analyzing a source. See pages 78-80 for an in-depth explanation and illustration of analytical writing.

PLAGIARISM

WHAT IT IS

Plagiarism can take many forms, and some are worse than others. Most simply, it means taking something that is not yours (an idea, a statistic, a piece of research, or an entire paper) and presenting it as your own. This is intellectual theft, and it violates everything that colleges and universities value.

HOW TO AVOID IT

To begin with, try to find a topic for your research that you care about. I realize that this is sometimes difficult, since many professors choose and/or limit your topics. If you can't choose your own topic, find some aspect of the topic that is meaningful to you. When you care about your subject, you're more likely to want to do your own thinking about it.

PLAGIARISM AND RESEARCH

As you do your research, try to be organized with your sources. Highlight passages that you plan on quoting, paraphrasing, or summarizing. Develop a number or symbol system to help you keep track of sources. I've seen far too many students suffer because they put off doing their in-text citations until they finished writing their papers; this is a terrible idea because at that stage you then have to look up all the sources (and sometimes even the page numbers) again. Maintain a system as you take notes and as you write. When in doubt, give credit to a source; if you're not sure whether or not you need an in-text citation, provide one.

QD

chapter 5

WRITING A PAPER

The work will teach you how to do it.

~ Estonian Proverb

WHY DO YOU HAVE TO WRITE PAPERS?

TO GET A GRADE

Of course this is why you write papers, but if you're only writing for a grade, you're unlikely to do your best work. Writing formal papers is an important part of college for some good reasons, like these:

IT MAKES YOU SMARTER

A confession: When I was a college student majoring in philosophy, I never enjoyed writing papers. I loved seeing the connections among ideas, and how one philosopher's thinking extended or transformed someone else's work, but I often dreaded the writing. I'd done all the important work of learning about a subject, so why did I have to write about it?

I came to understand, slowly, that it was in the writing that I was really learning how to make sense of what I'd read. Don't get me wrong—I love the idea of reading purely for pleasure. But at the heart of higher education is a different way of interacting with ideas. And that kind of interaction requires writing.

In short, some of our most significant learning takes place when we write.

IT IMPROVES THE WORLD

In Chapter 2, I said that all writing is rhetorical, meaning that at some level it is always trying to persuade the reader to accept the view(s) of the writer.

When a piece of writing is published as an essay or book, it becomes part of what might be called a "larger conversation," and it's in this conversation that writers have the power to improve the world. For example, when Michael Pollan wrote *The Omnivore's Dilemma*, about how agriculture works in America, he was continuing an ongoing conversation about how farms, industry, business, the environment, the oil industry, and our dining rooms are connected. Plenty of people disagreed with him—but in that disagreement, too, the conversation continued. Pollan doesn't get the last word in the conversation, but he's now part of it, and as a result, people are talking about these issues in new ways. In a not-so-small way, Pollan has changed the world.

Of course, when you write a paper for a college class, that paper isn't likely to be published and influence how people think about a subject. But if you try to think in those terms, it might help you write more purposeful papers.

EXTENDING THE CONVERSATION

First, you might notice that I'm reversing the concepts that I discussed in the previous chapter: "Here's what someone else has to say" and "Here's what I have to say about that." The reversal is because here I'm highlighting the fact that a paper needs to fundamentally be *your* ideas rather than those of your sources.

Your reader (that mythical stranger who is interested in your subject matter but doesn't know you—and is not your professor) has two basic expectations about your paper:

1. You have something to say.

> This means that your paper is driven by an idea that is at least somewhat new or original. It can't simply say what has been said before—why bother writing it if someone else already has?

2. You are aware of what has already been said.

In order for an intelligent reader to trust you, you must demonstrate that you're familiar with the important work that has been already been done on your subject.

If you think of any particular subject—global warming, the effects of technology on higher education, or how Millennials are changing the workplace—you can easily imagine it as a "conversation." One observer says one thing; another person responds to it, perhaps disagrees. Another commentator comes along and enters the conversation by disagreeing with both of the previous thinkers. And so on. The conversation moves in new directions, considers new evidence, continues to evolve. Sometimes the conversation becomes angry and unpleasant, but it's still a conversation. No one ever has the last word.

It's easy to see how this way of thinking about writing and research has implications beyond the classroom. Only in a country that preserves real intellectual freedom can ideas be debated so freely. By extension, when your professors require you to write a paper, they are asking you to participate in one of the most important forms of democracy available to us: the ability to think freely and share ideas.

Every day we read the work of professional writers in newspapers, magazines, and books. Because we only see  the finished product—the thing that has been revised and edited (often numerous times)—we might think that the writer simply sat down and typed it. I can assure you that this is almost never the case. Even the most gifted writers have to revise. In most cases, the finished product that we read has little in common with the writer's first draft. Certainly, writing comes more naturally to some people than others. But even for those people, writing is rarely easy, and it almost never comes without effort.

This chapter offers some advice about the writing process, but it's worth remembering that good writers rarely follow the steps exactly as I outline them. Instead, they tend to write in a way that has been described as *recursive*—meaning, roughly, that they go both forward and backward. They might go from brainstorming to drafting and back to brainstorming. Then, they might choose to revise a small portion of their writing so that it says exactly what they want it to, then go back to drafting again. Here's the basic process, in the order I'll discuss it in this chapter:

1. Find and narrow your topic
2. Brainstorm
3. Determine your purpose / create a tentative thesis
4. Make an outline
5. Write a draft
6. Revise
7. Proofread

Note: I'm assuming that you've already done some reading and research to prepare for the writing.

PRE-WRITING

FIND YOUR TOPIC

All of your college writing begins with some kind of assignment—it's smart to pay close attention to it. Make sure you know what's expected of you, and reread the assignment occasionally when you're in the process of writing the paper. If your topic has been assigned to you, skip to the next page.

THREE SUGGESTIONS

- Think about which class sessions you found most interesting. Go back and look at your notes for controversial issues, important commentators on the subject, etc.

- Freewrite about the broad subject—write down anything that comes to mind, including your own memories, observations, personal experiences. The goal at this stage is merely to find a possible direction for your research, one that, ideally, you care about personally.

- Explore the subject in articles, databases, or books (see Chapter 7 for guidelines). Don't think of this as research yet; instead, think of it simply as a way of exploring the subject in order to find a workable topic. But do keep track of sources you find in case you want to come back to them later when you do have a topic.

NARROW YOUR TOPIC

Start with a basic principle: If people have written entire books about your topic, it's not narrow enough. For example, when I started working on the sample paper in Chapter 8, I started with the broad topic of technology and higher education; then, after doing some freewriting and more reading, I decided to focus on classroom policies around the use of laptops, phones, and tablets—but *not* to narrow it even further to the issue of note-taking by hand versus on a laptop.

BRAINSTORM

The key to brainstorming is to learn how to outsmart your brain. (See "Your Brain as Obstacle" on page 72 for more on why this is necessary.) Two techniques—freewriting and clustering—are often helpful when you're trying to generate ideas or find direction for your writing.

MAPPING / CLUSTERING

This technique is good for people who are visual. It can be done on a piece of paper (the larger the better), but it is often most successful when done on a big board with many people contributing.

As with other forms of brainstorming, the key is to not limit the flow of ideas. Still, there's a little more critical thinking involved in clustering because it does depend on making logical connections among ideas.

Here's how it works. Start with any topic—try to express it in a single word, or two words at most. For this example, I'll use *education*. (See next page.) Next, think of ways to divide that subject into many parts, aspects, or issues—maybe ask yourself some of the "reporter's questions" later in the chapter.

FREEWRITING

One of the simplest ways to generate ideas for a paper is freewriting. The basic idea of freewriting is this: Write (or type—whichever you can do faster and most easily) quickly and without worrying about whether your ideas are good or whether they make sense. Don't worry about grammar. This isn't writing that you'll turn in—it's just a way to help you explore your interests, narrow your topic, and discover some possible questions about your topic.

CLUSTERING / MAPPING

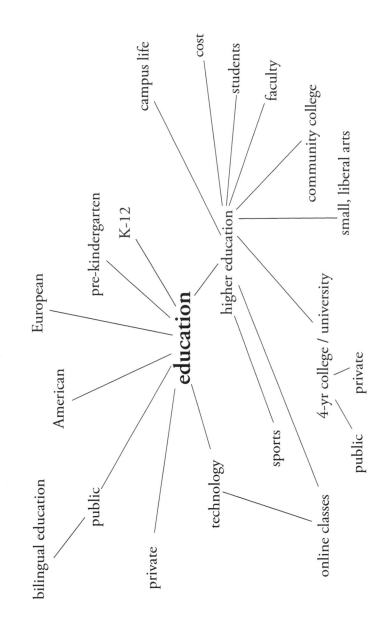

A couple of things to notice: If your "web" starts to move in one direction (as mine does toward higher education issues), you might start over with "higher education" in the middle and begin branching out again. Also, think about how pieces of this web could be connected. Combining technology, cost, and online classes, for example, could lead to a good topic about how these issues are changing college life.

What to do when you're freewriting

- Ask questions about your topic
- Try to connect different parts of the topic that interest you
- Answer some of the reporter's questions on the next page

What *not* to do when you're freewriting

- Worry about grammar or spelling
- Edit yourself
- Delete anything

ASK YOURSELF THE "REPORTER'S QUESTIONS"

The reporter's five "W" questions (there's also an "H") can help you break a big topic down into smaller parts. These questions can also help you make connections among the parts. Here's an example of applying the reporter's questions to the topic of education:

Who   Students, professors, administrators, parents, school boards, legislators

What   Private vs. public, pre-Kindergarten, grade school, high school, higher education

When   Different time periods, such as 18th century, early 20th century, 1970s, the future, etc.

Where   Rural versus urban or suburban schools, American versus European or other geographic regions, traditional vs. online

Why   Origins of education: Why did education become "formalized"? Why do we have compulsory education? Why is a college degree so important to employers, or is this changing?

How   Methods of educating people: whole langue versus phonics, or lecture versus "student-centered" instruction

FINAL THOUGHTS ON BRAINSTORMING

You'd be surprised how often something useful can come out of what seems like a bad idea. Some of the best ideas come after initially thinking, *That can't possibly work.*

Think about how creative many kids are—they invent games and "pretend" worlds all the time. Why? Because their imaginations are not limited by some "higher" voice telling them that their games are useless or poorly constructed. They just adapt the games, refine them, discard them, and so on. But they keep inventing.

Invention comes largely from a sense of play and often from lucky accidents. If you follow the rules all the time, the imaginative and inventive parts of your brain will never get a chance to function. And even though writing a paper for a class is not typically thought of as a creative act, there is still invention and creativity in the form of the kinds of connections (synthesis) you make.

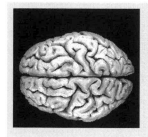 Your brain is powerful—it stores memories, processes emotions, perceives the world, and reasons. It can be infinitely creative, but it can also be a source of self-criticism. Be aware of this latter tendency when you're at the beginning of the writing process; you need to allow your mind to roam freely without having your inner critic shut down ideas and possibilities.

DECIDE ON YOUR PURPOSE

This is not quite the same as creating a thesis (see page 74 for that), though the two are closely connected. When I suggest that you think clearly about your purpose, I mean that you need to know what kind of paper you're writing.

You don't want to write a paper that's merely a report. That might have been acceptable in some high school classes, but it's not what most of your college profesors will be looking for. There are some exceptions, such as in the sciences, for example, where you may routinely be asked to write lab reports. These don't typically call for your interpretation or reflection—they want you to report on what you did and how you did it.

In terms of academic writing, most papers are informative, argumentative, or persuasive. To demonstrate, I'll use the topic of sleep deprivation. For each example, I'll offer a simple thesis statement that could work for that type of paper.

Informative

Sleep deprivation has serious consequences for college students.

An informative paper on this topic would likely examine the nature of sleep deprivation; it might include some history on human sleep patterns and consider competing perspectives (from biology, psychology, etc.) on *how* sleep deprivation can affect people, and how these effects might apply specifically to college students. It's important to note the difference between an informative paper and a mere report. An informative paper makes a claim which is then backed up with evidence and examples. It should also examine issues from a variety of perspectives.

Argumentative

Sleep deprivation can be a matter of life and death for doctors—and patients.

This paper would share some explanatory elements with an informative paper, but the primary difference is that it would seek to convince the reader to accept the writer's conviction that sleep deprivation is an important issue in the health care system. It's argumentative because some readers may not agree that this is an important problem; their position might be, "Well, everyone would like to get more sleep; at least doctors make a lot of money." It's the writer's job, then, to convince the reader that this is a serious issue.

Persuasive

Local police departments should offer new scheduling options since sleep deprivation can be a matter of life and death for police officers.

Again, this type of paper shares features with informative and argumentative papers. The key difference is that a persuasive paper asks the reader to adopt a specific position that could produce some change in the world.

CREATE A THESIS STATEMENT

Once you have some direction for your paper, you should start working on a thesis. (This isn't always true—in some cases, it makes more sense to begin with questions and uncertainties and allow yourself to discover the thesis later.)

Topic vs. thesis

Your topic is what the paper is about; your thesis is what you have to say *about* the topic. It's your position, your stance. Readers can't disagree with you about your topic, but some should be able to disagree with you about your thesis.

> **TOPIC:** Portable electronic devices (phones, laptops, etc.) in college classes

How would a reader disagree with that? He couldn't say, "That topic doesn't exist." Well, he could, but he'd be wrong; when you think of "the reader," you have to imagine a sane, rational person. So you have to add something to your topic that can give a reader something to disagree with:

> **THESIS:** The presence of portable electronic devices in college classrooms has changed the way students and professors interact.

Not many people would argue with this, of course, but an argument against this assertion is possible. Therefore, it's an acceptable thesis statement. If your professor wants a more argumentative paper, your thesis could look like this:

> **BETTER THESIS:** The presence of portable electronic devices in college classrooms has adversely affected the way students and professors interact.

Keys to a good thesis

- take a position
- open up a discussion or continue a "conversation"
- be specific and sufficiently narrow

PAUSE (AND DON'T FORGET TO READ)

You should know that the writing process rarely works as neatly as I'm attempting to lay it out here. Frequently, for example, you won't come up with a thesis statement until you've done some research or even drafted parts of your paper.

The process of developing a thesis, creating an outline, and writing a draft tend to get jumbled together.

Most importantly, don't forget to read and re-read your source material. I sometimes see students working on papers without also looking at a book, handout, or article online. This is a big mistake. You should be constantly examining your sources and thinking about how to use them.

WHO IS YOUR AUDIENCE?

You might be thinking: *This is easy—my audience is the professor.* In the practical sense, yes, you are writing *for* your professor. She might be the only one who will actually read the paper, and she's certainly the one who will be judging (grading) it.

Still, you'll write better papers if you try to think of a real audience. Consider the example of the persuasive purpose on the previous page: Local police departments should offer new scheduling options since sleep deprivation can be a matter of life and death for police officers.

If you think of your town's residents as your audience, it may help you write more purposefully. You still need to keep your voice academic, but just having an actual audience in mind often helps you think through the issues more clearly.

WORK FROM AN OUTLINE

At some point in the writing process, it's smart to write at least a basic, informal outline, like this:

1. Introduction, with thesis statement
2. Major point #1
3. Major point #2
4. Major point #3
5. Conclusion

You can have as many "major points" as you want—and each one isn't necessarily one paragraph. As you write longer papers, those major points will most likely be sections with multiple paragraphs. The main purpose for writing an outline is to be sure you know what each part of your paper is doing (and that you're not just saying the same thing in slightly different ways).

Here's an example of a more formal outline for the paper that starts on page 152. A formal outline uses uses Roman numerals and letters. One of the most basic rules is that if you have a 1 (or an A), you must have a 2 (or a B).

I. Introduction

    A. People don't like change

    B. Different approaches to classroom policy

    C. Thesis: Professors need to be more flexible about devices in class

II. Rights of students

    A. They are adults

    B. They're paying

III. Students sometimes need devices

    A. Emergencies

    B. Better concentration

IV. Naysayer: Boredom (see page 80 for more on naysayers)

    A. Most uses of devices not legitimate

    B. Counter to naysayer

        1. Problem is boring lectures

        2. texting has no effect on learning (source)

V. Naysayer: Distraction to *other* students

    A. View of distracted students *causes* distraction (source)

    B. Counter to naysayer

        1. Have students on devices sit in back?

        2. Students sign pledge?

VI. Students with disabilities

    A. Legal issue: ADA rights

    B. Ethical issue: Violation of privacy

    C. Possible solution?

VII. Conclusion

    A. Humans will adapt

    B. Devices will eventually win (in college classrooms)

SAVE YOUR WORK

Before you even start writing a draft, remember to save your work as you go. I strongly recommend using a free cloud service like Dropbox. See page 214.

WRITE A DRAFT

If you're having trouble getting started with a draft, try writing one of your body paragraphs first. More specifically, start writing a body paragraph you *know* will be part of your paper, and one you feel pretty confident about. Beyond just helping you get your draft started, this has another advantage: In some cases, what you think will just be one paragraph or section of your paper will actually grow into multiple paragraphs once you start writing.

Another reason to start writing your body paragraphs before your introduction is because it's often helpful to know everything that will be in the paper before you try to introduce that material.

In short, there's no single correct way to write a draft—but very few writers start at the beginning and write straight through to the end. Most will jump from one part of the paper to another, and then decide how all the pieces fit together later. The best piece of advice I've heard about drafting: Instead of staring at a blank page waiting for inspiration to come, lower your standards and start writing.

TOPIC SENTENCES

Good topic sentences make it much easier for your reader to follow your thinking, but they also have an important function for you as the writer—they help ensure that *you* know what you're doing in every single paragraph of your essay. Writing a clear topic sentence forces you to decide what you're trying to accomplish in a given paragraph, and it might also help you eliminate (or move elsewhere) material that doesn't fit with the topic sentence.

Consider an example related to that topic of sleep deprivation. Let's imagine that one body paragraph will focus on how sleep deprivation affects the body. Here's a barely adequate topic sentence, one that would likely lead to a paragraph that feels more like a report:

Sleep deprivation has many effects on the body.

Here's a better topic sentence, one that would connect to the informative thesis statement I discussed a few pages back ("Sleep deprivation has serious consequences for college students"):

College students should be aware of how sleep deprivation may affect their bodies.

The next step is to consider what you do after that topic sentence, and this is where you need to know how to write *analytically*.

ANALYTICAL WRITING

Your professors will often say that they want you to write analytically, so what exactly does it mean to analyze something? Here are three definitions:

- to study something in a systematic and careful way

- to study or examine something in detail in order to understand or explain it

- to separate (a thing, idea, etc.) into its parts so as to find out their nature, proportion, function, interrelationship, etc.

Some combination of all three of those gets at what you're likely to be doing when you write analytically.

Let's return to the example of sleep deprivation and the topic sentences above. First, an example of the kind of writing that is *not* analytical:

NO   Sleep deprivation has many effects on the body. It can cause "hallucinations, psychosis, and long-term memory impairment" (Maxon). One study at Harvard University says that sleep deprivation can lead to hypertension (O'Connor), which is also known as high blood pressure. Hypertension can lead to a number of heart problems, including "coronary artery disease, stroke, heart failure, peripheral vascular disease, vision loss, and chronic kidney disease" ("Hypertension").

That's not a terrible paragraph. It shows that the writer did some research and documented their sources properly—but it's mere information with no clear purpose. It offers the reader nothing more than weakly connected facts.

It's also worth noting that the paragraph has no transitions, and this is often a good indication that the writer is not revealing how ideas connect to each other. (See pages 82-83 for more on transitions.)

By contrast, if we start with a broader purpose (for the entire paper) of illustrating how sleep deprivation is a problem for college students, a body paragraph of that paper might logically want to address the effects on the body. In this case, I decided to focus on a specific concern, namely, the possibility of gaining weight as a result of insufficient sleep. I decided to pursue this specific issue because I found quite a bit of research on this subject.

YES **1** Students who don't get enough sleep also risk gaining weight. **2** Most of the research suggests that this is because being sleep deprived can alter your eating patterns, often leading to overeating. **3** According to Chris Winter, a doctor who runs Charlottesville Neurology and Sleep Medicine, "If the brain is not getting the energy it needs from sleep it will often try to get it from food" (qtd. in Swalin). **4** A 2004 study revealed that one of the key culprits may be gherlin, the "hunger hormone"; subjects who had reduced sleep tended to experience an increase in gherlin, which the researchers determined was "likely to increase appetite, possibly explaining the increased BMI observed with short sleep duration" (Taheri et al.).

This paragraph could use more development and examples, but it should give you an idea how to use and interact with source material purposefully. What makes it analytical?

1 Topic sentence

2 The second sentence summarizes findings from a number of different studies; this intellectual act is, by its nature, analytical because it involves synthesizing information.

3 The third sentence moves to a somewhat general assertion from a source that backs up the basic idea of the paragraph.

4 The fourth sentence moves to a possible explanation, one that is specific and which introduces us to a new term (gherlin).

What I've described above is a basic form of analytical writing. The next step is to *complicate* the information. By complicate I mean that you want to show some subtle differences in how your subject matter is being addressed by your sources. Primarily, this means looking for where they arrive at different explanations or interpretations of an issue.

Here's one way to follow up on the paragraph above while moving in a slightly different direction (this would likely be a new paragraph):

YES   Other researchers believe that the core problem is in the brain itself. Matthew P. Walker, a professor of psychology and neuroscience at the University of California, Berkeley, describes the effect of sleep deprivation as a "double hit" on the brain (qtd. in O'Connor). He notes that on reduced sleep, subjects were more susceptible to fatty foods and sweets, which "stimulated stronger responses in a part of the brain that helps govern the motivation to eat." This is the first of the two "hits," while the second is to the frontal cortex, the part of the brain associated with impulse control. In short, when we're sleep deprived, the brain desires foods that are bad for us, and we have less ability to control that desire.

Yes, all the information is from the same source—and in case you were wondering, it's not necessary to repeat "qtd. in O'Connor" because it's clear that I'm using the same source.

One last thought on this paragraph. The final sentence is a good example of purposeful restatement, which serves two purposes. For your reader, it helps clarify and simplify some complex material. For your professor, especially in a writing course, it shows that you understand the nuances of your research.

The concept of the *naysayer* comes from someone who says "nay"—or no, to use today's language. Whatever position you take in a paper, you should be asking yourself, "Who would say *no* to this, and why?"

INTRODUCE NAYSAYERS

It might seem like a bad idea to introduce an idea that could contradict your argument, but it actually makes your position stronger. In fact, if you don't deal with obvious objections to your views, your readers often think of those objections, causing them to wonder if you're avoiding a complication because you don't know how to deal with it. Worse still, some readers might question your "ethos" (see page 22) if they think that certain complications haven't even occurred to you. In short, your credibility is at stake.

See pages 155, 183 and 186 for examples of how to incorporate naysayers into an essay.

"I" STATEMENTS / FIRST PERSON: PROCEED WITH CAUTION

I think / I believe / It is my opinion / The point I am making is

Many professors don't allow students to use first person . . . for two reasons: first, they say that students who rely on "I think" (and its variants) tend to make personal claims rather than clearly reasoned points; second, many professors argue that the first person simply isn't necessary, as in this case:

> I believe that George Will's definition of reality television is too narrow, and that he ignores many compelling and worthwhile programs that use the "reality" format.

Eliminating the first few words results in a more efficient sentence that doesn't lose any clarity:

> George Will's definition of reality television is too narrow, and he ignores many compelling and worthwhile programs that use the "reality" format.

But other professors . . . encourage their students to use first person ("I") in some circumstances. They argue that it's good for you to use these constructions as a way of making clear—both for yourself as the writer and for your readers—what you are saying. Furthermore, using the "I" as I demonstrate below can help differentiate your ideas from those that come from your sources. For example, let's imagine that you've just paraphrased an assertion from one of your sources:

> George Will characterizes the emergence of reality television as the end of Western civilization.

In your next sentence, you want to challenge that idea. Using an "I" statement helps the reader shift gears—from thinking about George Will's idea to focusing on yours:

> **I would argue,** however, that Will's definition of reality television is too narrow, and that he ignores many compelling and worthwhile programs that use the "reality" format.

(The transitional word *however* also helps the reader make the shift.)

CREATE TRANSITIONS

BETWEEN PARAGRAPHS

When your reader goes from one paragraph of your paper to the next, it's important that you help them make that shift. You need to make it easy to see how the ideas in one paragraph connect to those in the next, and that's the job of your transition.

The example below, from the sample paper in Chapter 9, shows the final sentence of a paragraph that discusses students who don't pay attention during class due to the distraction of phones or laptops. The next paragraph moves to a new idea. (Transitional elements have been removed to illustrate the point.)

> . . . This is why many colleges have been actively trying to help faculty develop more engaging ways of delivering their material—so that students will pay attention.
>
> Professors are concerned that one student's use of a device can be distracting to other students.

There's no transition between the two paragraphs, but it's pretty easy to create a link between those ideas. The simplest way to do it is to use an idea from the last sentence of the first paragraph, briefly, in the first sentence of the next paragraph.

> . . . This is why many colleges have been actively trying to help faculty develop more engaging ways of delivering their material—so that students will pay attention.
>
> For many professors, **the key issue is not whether individual students are giving the professor their full attention**; they are concerned that one student's use of a device can be distracting to other students.

The strategy is simple: summarize the basic idea of the previous paragraph, briefly, and then connect to it. But it can still be better with a couple of transition words added:

> For many professors, **though**, the key issue is not whether individual students are giving the professor their full attention; **instead**, they are concerned that one student's use of a device can be distracting to other students.

The transitional words *though* and *instead* both help the reader shift in the opposite direction from the previous paragraph. These are small elements, but they are immensely beneficial to your reader. You can read this in context in the sample paper on page 187. Note: I've switched these citations to MLA style.

TRANSITIONAL WORDS / PHRASES

SIMILARITY		CAUSE AND EFFECT
likewise		accordingly
similarly		consequently
also		hence
too		so
just as		thus
		therefore

SUPPORT
additionally
also
as well
equally important
further
furthermore
in addition
moreover

CONTRAST
but
however
in contrast
on the other hand
whereas
on the contrary
nevertheless
still
yet

EMPHASIS
certainly
even
indeed
in fact
of course
truly

EXAMPLE
for example
for instance
namely
specifically
to illustrate

BETWEEN AND WITHIN SENTENCES

Many writers assume that transitions appear only in the first sentence of a new paragraph, but you need them between—and within—sentences too. Here's another part of the sample essay from Chapter 9. (Transitional elements have been removed to illustrate the point.)

> . . . They found that when students took notes on a laptop—in the "encoding" phase of learning—they were not processing the information well because they tended to rely on "verbal transcription" (8). They were simply typing what they heard rather than thinking about the information. Students who took notes by hand were forced to be more selective about what they wrote down, leading to a higher level of processing.

As it is now, that reads like a series of disconnected facts. To connect them, think about how the ideas relate to one another. The middle sentence is a restatement of the research findings. The final sentence takes the reader in a different direction, so it needs a contrasting transition.

> . . . They found that when students took notes on a laptop—in the "encoding" phase of learning—they were not processing the information well because they tended to rely on "verbal transcription" (8). **In other words**, they were simply typing what they heard rather than thinking about the information. **By contrast**, students who took notes by hand were forced to be more selective about what they wrote down, leading to a higher level of processing.

CREATE A GOOD TITLE

It can be difficult to come up with a good title, but I encourage you to spend at least a few minutes brainstorming different possibilities. It's the very first thing your reader will see, and a bland title won't make much of an impression.

There's a simple formula for the titles of many academic papers: start with something interesting and slightly mysterious, then follow it with a more conventional phrase or clause that clarifies what your paper is actually doing.

Something Creative and Intriguing:

Something Standard That Makes Clear What Your Paper Will Investigate

REVISE

First drafts are rarely very good. They are a starting point, little more. I'll offer a few suggestions about revision below, but if you have a complete draft, it's often difficult to assess it accurately on your own. In short, this is an excellent time to make a visit to the Writing Center.

If you're tackling the revision on your own, start by writing down the following, briefly:

- What is the purpose / thesis of the paper? (State it in one simple sentence.)

- What does each body paragraph do to help support or develop the thesis? (State each paragraph's purpose in a brief phrase.)

If you write down the answers to those two questions, what you see should look roughly like an outline. By the way, if you decided not to write an outline before drafting, you really should write a simple one before revising. Once you can see the major parts of your paper broken down into brief phrases, it's much easier to assess if the parts are logically connected. Doing this should also reveal if two paragraphs or sections of the paper say almost exactly the same thing—that's a clear sign that you need to rethink your organization.

Revision does not mean to "fix" your draft. **MYTH: REVISION IS EASY**
It's more than simply finding the errors and
correcting them. The word itself, *revise*, has its roots in the idea of sight, and
suggests "seeing again," or seeing your work in a new way. First and foremost,
you want to rethink your ideas—how they connect, how you express them,
and what, in the larger sense, they say about your topic.

PROOFREAD

See pages 93-94.

FIRST IMPRESSIONS

It may seem odd to bring up first impressions as one of the final items in this
chapter, but it's here for a reason—to give you something to think about before
you turn in your paper. I assume that your time and energy are limited, so I
know that in many cases you won't be able to revise as thoroughly as you'd like
to. My advice here is to put the time you do have into some key elements at the
beginning of your paper. If you get off to a good start, your professors are much
more inclined to forgive the things that don't go quite as well later in the paper.
In order, here's where I think you should focus your energies:

1. **Introduction:** Start with a good "hook" that grabs the reader's attention.

2. **Thesis statement:** Make sure it's clear and as well-written as possible.

3. **Title:** Get creative (see previous page).

4. **First body paragraph:** Make sure it has a clear and purposeful topic
    sentence and that you present good evidence from quality sources; get
    your citations right.

5. **Other body paragraphs**

6. **Conclusion:** Try not to simply repeat what you wrote in the introduction.

QD

chapter 6

EDITING & PROOFREADING

*The difference between the right word and the almost right word
is the difference between lightning and the lightning bug.*
> ~ Mark Twain

I believe more in the scissors than I do in the pencil.
> ~ Truman Capote

Does this scenario sound familiar? You've waited until the day before a paper is due to start working on it. You stay up until three in the morning to finish it, get a few hours sleep, finish the works-cited page, give it a title, and print it. You rush to campus, make it to class just in time, and triumphantly hand in your paper.

Then, when you get the paper back, you see that the professor has marked several mistakes you could've found if you'd left yourself more time. And the grade reflects all those careless mistakes.

In my class, a sloppy paper with more than a couple of careless errors will rarely get a grade above a C. On the other hand, I'm aware that sometimes it's all you can do simply to get a paper finished at all, and in those cases, I'm pleased that you got the assignment done, even if it's not your best work. Getting a slightly lower grade is always better than getting no grade.

The point here is to remind you how important it is to make your paper as "clean" as you can. Ideally, you'd finish it at least a couple of days before it's due—because you always see errors and problems after a day or so of not looking at the paper. If you have time, it's always a good idea to take your near-final draft to the Writing Center too.

A few suggestions for both editing and proofreading

- Work from a printed copy of your paper—it's easier to see problems.

- Read your paper out loud, slowly.

- Read your paper backwards, one sentence at a time. This is useful because it disrupts your usual flow and forces you to focus on each sentence individually. This is particularly helpful if you have grammatical errors.

- Ask a friend to read it and mark obvious problems. If your friend is a good writer, ask them to make other sentence-level suggestions too. Even better, have your friend read the paper out loud to you. Listen for places where they have trouble reading fluidly, which can indicate problems with rhythm and emphasis.

EDITING

When you're writing a first draft of a paper, you don't want to take too much time trying to make your sentences perfect. At that stage, it's more important to get all your ideas down and in a logical order.

Once you've done that, though, then you want to edit your work. By this, I mean that you put all of your energy into making your sentences as clear and fluid as you can.

VAGUE LANGUAGE: IT, THIS, THINGS, ETC.

My colleague Elizabeth Trobaugh strictly limits the use of the word *this* in student papers. Her opposition to the word is well-reasoned: Writers frequently fail to be clear what words like *it, this, things,* and *issues* refer to. Or they have a vague idea but don't take the time to be specific about the reference. Here's an example from a recent student paper:

> So maybe other cultures have **things** we don't. Sometimes they are heavily valued, other times not so much. In **this** case **it** is.

What *things*? In *which* case *what* is? Be specific. As a writer, your job is to make it as easy as possible for the reader to understand what you have to say. (I can't even offer you a revised version of that sentence because I don't know what, exactly, the writer was trying to say.)

Here's an example I can revise, from a student essay about obesity in America:

> David Zinczenko grew up with a "daily choice between McDonalds, Taco Bell, and Kentucky Fried Chicken." He believes that **it** isn't the eater's fault. **It'**s the issue that fast food restaurants are everywhere and Americans have no choice, but to eat **it**.

Revised:

> David Zinczenko grew up with a "daily choice between McDonalds, Taco Bell, and Kentucky Fried Chicken." He believes that **teen obesity** isn't the eater's fault. Because fast food restaurants are everywhere, Americans have no choice but to eat **unhealthy foods**.

THERE IS / THERE ARE

These constructions are a poor way to begin a sentence—they tend to be weak because they allow you to avoid saying anything about your subject. For example:

> **There is** a reason why good writers avoid empty phrases.

What's the reason? Why not tell us in the same sentence?

> Good writers avoid empty phrases because readers resent being forced to read unnecessary words.

"TO BE" VERBS

One of my high school teachers made us write an entire paper without using any "to be" verbs. In other words, we couldn't use *am, is, was, were, are, been, being,* or *be.* It's difficult not to use these verb forms because they're the most common verbs in the English language. (In that sentence, I used two: It *is* difficult, and they *are* the most common....)

I wouldn't suggest that you try to eliminate *all* of these verbs in your writing, but it can be helpful to replace as many of them as possible with stonger, more expressive verbs. Here's an example, using my sentence from above:

> It's difficult not to use these verb forms because . . . .

As I thought about how to get rid of that first *is*, I couldn't just think of a synonym for *is difficult*. I had to think about the entire concept and try to express it differently. Here's what I came up with, and it's no accident that I think the revision is superior:

> We rely on these verb forms because . . . .

Or, if you didn't want to use *We* :

> Writers rely on these verb forms because . . . .

USING DASHES

The dash is a way of separating information. The key difference between the dash and other "separating" marks of punctuation (commas, semi-colons, periods) is that the dash is a stronger interruption, and it generally feels less formal than those other marks. A word on what a dash is *not*: a hyphen. A hyphen is a punctuation mark that connects two or more words: re-create, ex-wife, door-to-door salesman.

Like other marks of punctuation, the dash has grammatical rules that apply to it. These rules depend on whether you use a single dash or a pair, so I'll discuss these separately.

A dash always calls some attention to itself, so you should use it sparingly. It's particularly useful when your sentence includes a number of commas; the dash, or paired dashes, can help keep the grammar of your sentence clear.

Single dash

> Emily walked away from the restaurant—and away from an entire way of life.

Here, the dash allows you to add another piece of information to the sentence. It could have been done with a comma instead of a dash, but the dash provides more emphasis. It gives the second part of the sentence more weight and importance. A single dash can also allow the part after the dash to function as a definition (not in a dictionary sense) or explanation of what precedes it, as in the next three examples, all from Hanna Rosen's article, "The Touch-Screen Generation":

> They made a list of the blockbusters over the decades—the first Tonka trucks, the Frisbee, the Hula-Hoop, the Rubik's Cube.

In that sentence, what comes after the dash gives examples of the blockbusters; Rosin could also have used a colon (:) instead of the dash. A comma in place of the dash, though, would have made the sentence confusing because of the three commas that separate the toys. The dash is the perfect choice here.

Here's another example from the same article; in this usage, the dash allows the writer to add information and call attention to it.

> The gathering was organized by Warren Buckleitner, a longtime reviewer of interactive children's media who likes to bring together developers, researchers, and interest groups—and often plenty of kids, some still in diapers.

There's one other way that a single dash can be used, and it's a bit unusual grammatically in that it allows the writer to connect two complete thoughts:

> Also, they were not really meant to teach you something specific—they existed mostly in the service of having fun.

In that sentence, the part that comes after the dash is a complete thought, which means that in this case the dash has the same grammatical "power" as a period or semicolon.

Paired dashes

When you use dashes in a pair, remember that they function almost exactly like parentheses. Grammatically, the principle is identical: Whatever you put inside the dashes can be removed without affecting the grammar of the sentence.

In terms of meaning, too, paired dashes resemble parentheses. What you find inside the dashes is something of an afterthought, an aside, something interesting but not essential to the sentence. What the paired dashes do that parentheses don't is call more attention to the information inside them. Parentheses are like a whispered comment, while dashes are like a poke in the ribs.

> ReD is one of a handful of consultancies that treat everyday life—and everyday consumerism—as a subject worthy of the scrutiny normally reserved for academic social science.
>
> — Graeme Wood, "Anthropology Inc.," *The Atlantic*, March 2013

The information inside the dashes here is an additional piece of information that's not critical to the sentence; however, in placing this brief phrase inside the dashes, the writer has brought more attention to the idea of consumerism.

Here's another example that works in a similar way.

> Still, given the food industry's power to tinker with and market food, we should not dismiss its ability to get unhealthy eaters—slowly, incrementally—to buy better food.
>
> – David H. Freedman, "How Junk Food Can End Obesity," *The Atlantic*, July 2013

And finally, an example of how paired dashes can help you create a lengthy, complex sentence.

> The study adds to a river of evidence suggesting that for the first time in modern history—and in spite of many health-related improvements in our environment, our health care, and our nondietary habits—our health prospects are worsening, mostly because of excess weight.
>
> – David H. Freedman, "How Junk Food Can End Obesity"

That sentence would be somewhat demanding for many readers, but I do think it holds together well—and it does so in large part because of its sophisticated use of dashes.

DIRECTNESS: AVOIDING STUPID WRITING

The worst kind of bad writing is that which tries to make itself sound smarter or more complex than it actually is, like this:

> Interest in the possible applicability of TRIZ tools and techniques to the world of management and organizational innovation issues continues to grow.

Some of you may be impressed by that—you may think it's sophisticated and complex. It's complicated, that's for sure. But only in the structure of the sentence, not in content. Using that sentence, I'll show you the four key principles for bad writing.

HOW TO WRITE BADLY IN FOUR SIMPLE STEPS

1. **Remove any human presence**: The sentence is "disembodied," which means that it doesn't have a "body," or person. The first word of the sentence is *interest*, so who's interested? Businesses, I assume, so why not say so? Some writers seem to think that if you remove human beings from sentences, the writing will sound smarter. But all it really does is make the sentence harder to understand.

2. **Turn verbs into nouns (also known as nominalization)**: *Applicability* is a nominalization of the verb *apply*; *innovation* is a nominalization of *innovate*.

3. **Use more words than you need**: *Possible* and *the world of* are not needed in this sentence.

4. **Move the verb as far away from the subject as you can**: The subject is *interest*, and the verb is *continues*; there are eighteen words between the two, which makes it extremely difficult to connect them. Our most basic desire in English sentences is for a subject and a verb, preferably close together.

* * *

The guiding principle of the writing in that TRIZ sentence is this: If it's hard to read, you must have to be smart in order to write it. Good writers know that this principle is wrong; furthermore, it reveals a contempt for the reader. When politicians and business owners communicate with you in this way, you should demand to know why they want to make their policies and practices harder rather than easier to understand. Do they have something to hide?

Here's how the TRIZ sentence could be written more clearly, without any loss of meaning:

> Businesses can become more innovative in management and organization when they apply TRIZ tools and techniques.

I'm not absolutely certain I've said what the original writer intended—but that's because their writing is unclear. At any rate, I think I'm close. And I've taken a sentence that was twenty-two words and reduced it to fifteen words (32 percent more efficient!); also, it has a real subject (businesses), followed immediately by a verb, and this combination of changes makes the sentence far easier to read.

English is a flexible, adaptable language, but when writers violate the principles that make it work, they create sentences that don't communicate effectively.

PROOFREAD

Proofreading isn't particularly difficult—you're not concerned with the big ideas at this stage, just the correctness of words and sentences. You want the paper to feel polished and professional, so check for spelling errors, missing words, quotation marks turned the wrong direction, anything that might communicate sloppiness to your reader.

FIND AND CORRECT OBVIOUS ERRORS

See Chapter 3 for common errors that you should be able to correct. Make sure, too, that you have not misspelled anyone's name; when you refer to Jane Smiley as *Jane Smily*, your professor will doubt your ability to pay close attention to details.

CUT USELESS WORDS AND PHRASES

I know, you're often trying to get *up* to your professor's minimum length requirement. And now I'm telling you to cut words. But it's worth it—professors appreciate crisply written prose that doesn't include wasted words. (I should, for example, change the end of that sentence to this: *doesn't waste words.*)

Useless words

Inexperienced writers often use a lot of words and phrases that don't add anything to their sentences. They're filler—get rid of them. The worst offenders are the first five, in bold.

really	individual	all things considered
very	specific	in a manner of speaking
basically	type of	as a matter of fact
actually	particular	definitely
kind of	in the process of	as it were
sort of	more or less	
generally	for the most part	

MORE WORDS THAT CAN REPLACE PHRASES

All of the words below in bold are appropriate for academic writing, whereas the words in the two columns to the right are often used when writers are trying to make their sentences sound more impressive—without actually *saying* anything impressive.

because	for the reason that the reason for due to the fact that in light of the fact that	on account of considering the fact that on the grounds that because of the fact that
when	on the occasion of under circumstances in which	in a situation in which
about	as regards with regard to where _____ is concerned	in reference to concerning the matter of
now / today	at this point in time in this day and age	at the present time
must / should	it is crucial that there is a need/necessity for	it is necessary that it is important that
can	is able to has the capacity for	has the opportunity to has the ability to
may / might	it is possible that it could happen that	there is a chance that the possibility exists for

THE DANGERS OF SPELL CHECK

Spell Check is useful, of course, but it doesn't replace common sense. For example, if you misspell *definitely* (as many people do), Spell Check will frequently offer *defiantly* as the first option to correct your error. But this is an entirely different word, with a very different meaning. If you blindly accept every suggestion Spell Check makes without thinking about the word, you're likely to end up with some ridiculous mistakes. As always, think for yourself.

QD

chapter 7

FINDING SOURCES

Research means that you don't know, but are willing to find out.

> ~ Charles Kettering

True genius resides in the capacity for evaluation of uncertain, hazardous, and conflicting information.

> ~ Winston Churchill

It's never been easier to find information on every topic imaginable. The problem now is that it's *too* easy, meaning that you can quickly become overwhelmed by too many sources. This chapter will help you find quality sources in a variety of ways—and offer you some tips for keeping track of those sources and getting a head start on documentation.

As you read the following pages, remember that often you'll want to combine research strategies. For example, let's say that you find what looks like a good source via Google Scholar—only to discover that you have to pay to read beyond the abstract. That's when you want to switch to a library database, where there's a good chance you'll find and be able to read the entire article.

GOOGLE*

* I've not been paid by Google to endorse any of their products. In fact, as part of my research for this chapter, I looked into alternative search engines. Two of the most popular were Bing and DuckDuckGo. I used the exact same search terms with those two services and got significantly worse results. In both cases, most of the results on the first page were links to stores selling laptops. Even one "article" that appeared further down the first page of results was part of a promotional site for a company selling marketing and advertising services to colleges.

So I'm sticking with Google, and for (basic) research purposes, I recommend that you do the same. If you're concerned about privacy, do a search for "turn off tracking." Or, at the very least, sign out of Google (assuming you have an account) before you search.

SEARCH TERMS

The first step in trying to find information about your topic is choosing search terms. It's fine to start with broad search terms, but it's smart to narrow your terms further as you search.

Throughout this chapter, I'll be sticking to one topic: the debate surrounding the use of laptops, phones and tablets in college classrooms. You can see two sample papers based on this research at the end of Chapters 8 and 9.

I began my search with the simplest terms: *laptops in classrooms*. Well, that's what I started to type into a Google search field, but as I'm sure you know, Google likes to predict what you're going to type. I encourage you to slow down and read through those predictions since you can frequently find good ways to narrow your topic or focus your research.

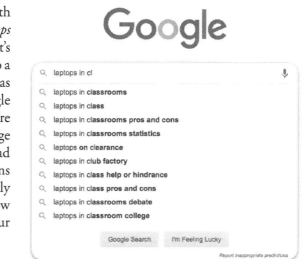

I hadn't planned on including the word *college*, but when I saw that Google was suggesting it, I realized that it would be dumb not to include it since I don't need to read articles about the use of technology in elementary schools.

ANALYZING SEARCH RESULTS

As you brose through the search results, you want to be able to quickly determine which sources might be useful—and which ones to stay away from. This is the first result from the search:

1 www.brookings.edu › research › for-better-learning-in-college-lecture... ▾

2 **For better learning in college lectures, lay down the laptop and ...**

3 Aug 10, 2017 - Students using **laptops** can also distract their classmates from their learning,

4 another lab experiment suggests. Researchers at York and McMaster recruited students to watch a lecture and then tested their comprehension.

1. **URL / Name of website.** As you gain more experience as a reader and researcher, you'll start to learn the names of some sites/publications that are reputable. For now, at least, keep in mind that .edu and .org sites are frequently better than .com sites. But not always—as you'll see on the next page.

2. **Name of article.** You can make some quick judgments about the likely quality of the article just by reading the title. Focus on the language and punctuation—avoid, for example, any title with excessive exclamation points or question marks. Contrast the title of this article with the one on the top of the next page.

3. **Date.** With many topics (like this one), you'll definitely want to find recent research. An article from, say, 2002, on technology in the college classroom was written before smartphones even existed.

4. **Text from article.** If nothing about the name of the website or article discouraged you, have a quick look at the preview of the text from the article. As I suggested above with the name of the article, think about the quality of the language here. If you want to use it as a source, it should sound relatively formal and professional—no slang, no sloppy writing. With this example, you can see that the article is citing other research, which is always a good sign.

WHAT YOU DON'T WANT TO SEE

medium.com › i-hate-when-teachers-tell-me-to-put-my-phone-away-7... ▾
I hate when teachers tell me to put my phone away - Ben ...
Mar 22, 2016 - Some classes won't see a single **laptop** or cell phone, due to that professor or ... I'm in a **classroom**, it's 11:58am and **class** starts at noon.

You might not have heard of medium.com, but I'm familiar with it. Anyone can create a page on medium.com, so it's a form of self-publishing. How is that different from other kinds of publishing? The main way is that if something is self-published, it typically has not been checked for accuracy (or logic or reasonableness) by anyone other than the writer. That work usually falls to editors, and without them, it's anything goes.

COMPARING RESULTS

Examine the four results below and think about how you would choose which articles to read or ignore, then have a look at my assessment on the next page.

1 www.chronicle.com › article › Should-You-Allow-Laptops-in ▾
Should You Allow Laptops in Class? Here's What the Latest ...
Feb 6, 2019 - So where does that leave us in the **laptops**-in-the-**classroom** debate? ... The Future of Learning: How **Colleges** Can Transform the Educational ...

2 www.npr.org › sections › 2018/01/24 › laptops-and-phones-in-the-class...
Laptops And Phones In The Classroom: Yea, Nay Or A Third ...
Jan 24, 2018 - "Beyond being distracting, students also use phones/**laptops**/devices as ... The **college classroom** is ... a unique space to exchange ideas and ...

3 www.scientificamerican.com › article › students-are-better-off-without... ▾
Students are Better Off without a Laptop in the Classroom ...
Jul 11, 2017 - As recent high school graduates prepare for their migration to **college** in the fall, one item is sure to top most students' shopping wish lists: a ...

4 www.panopto.com › blog › the-case-for-banning-laptops-in-classroo... ▾
The Case For Banning Laptops In Classrooms and ... - Panopto
Jun 11, 2019 - Dynarski goes on to say that, based on the results from these **college classroom** studies, she expects **laptops** and tablets similarly hurt ...

Here's where things get complicated.

1   The first result is from a .com site, but it's actually a very respected publication for people in higher education. Any of your professors would recognize its name, but how would you know that's a quality site? The word *chronicle* is somewhat old-fashioned, and maybe you've heard of it as the name of a newspaper (like the *San Francisco Chronicle*). The title of the article, though, should give you a hint that the audience for this publication is teachers and professors.

    Another plus is that the article is from February 2019, so it's quite recent.

2   You might have heard of NPR, but if not, it stands for National Public Radio, a taxpayer-supported media outlet. In short, it is a quality publication—which is not to say that it's always reliable and/or unbiased, but it's a far better source for good information than many other online sites. And since I'm looking at these results while thinking about how the source might be useful in my paper, I like the fact that the title of this one promises multiple ways of thinking about the subject ("Yea, Nay or a Third Way").

3   This is another publication you might be familiar with; if you're not, though, the title *Scientific American* should be more encouraging than, say, *medium.com*. And the language in the excerpt sounds formal, especially the phrase "migration to college." In other words, this would a source worth reading.

4   The last of these was unfamiliar to me. I thought it was a good sign that the excerpt appears to be quoting a source, but I was less enthusiastic about the fact that it is identified as a blog in the URL. Still, I thought it was worth clicking on and reading at least some of the article.

    The author (unnamed) addresses many of the standard concerns about distraction in the classroom, citing some of the same sources I've mentioned in this chapter—but the "article" ends with a sales pitch for Panopto's services: "Panopto is the easiest way to record, live stream, manage, and share videos across your organization." As a source, it doesn't bring anything new to the issue, and I don't like that it's trying to sell me something. Conclusion: I wouldn't use it in a paper.

CONTROLLING SEARCH DATES

If you're getting a lot of older articles in your search results, you can customize the dates. First, click on **Tools** on the right side of the search screen.

Then, click on the pull-down menu **Any time**.

At the bottom, choose **Custom range**.

Select the date range.

CREATING BETTER SEARCH TERMS

For many topics, it almost doesn't matter what search terms you use—you'll find good sources right away. If you don't get good results, though, here are a few ways to search more effectively.

Use an * (asterisk)

This tells Google to search for any form of the word *learn*: *learned*, *learning*, etc.

Use a - (hyphen / minus sign)

This will exclude results with the word after the minus sign. In the example below, my original search was for *college laptops phones*, and many of the results were links to reviews of laptops being recommended to college students, and most of them said something like "10 Best Laptops for College"—so I added *-best* to my search terms.

The results improved, but I still saw quite a few links to stores with laptops for sale, so I added *-sale*.

Q   college laptops phones -best -sale   🎤

Add as many as you like to get rid of results that aren't relevant to your search. Be aware that the minus sign won't work in most databases (where you'd use the word NOT).

Put a specific phrase inside quotes

Do this when you want to find a specific combination of words. The search below will only show results where those two words, *ban laptops*, appear together.

Q   professors "ban laptops"   🎤

Use the word OR

This increases the number of results because it looks for pages that have either of those words.

Q   laptops OR phones college   🎤

FOLLOW YOUR SOURCES

Once you have one good source, it frequently leads to others, particularly when your topic is something relatively current. In this case, I started with an article from the *New York Times*. Whatever you might think of the *Times* as a news source, it does publish a range of opinion pieces, and it's a good place to find commentary on a variety of issues—and not always from one political perspective.

In this article, the author is arguing that laptops have no place in college classrooms or meetings. Before I started reading, though, I scrolled down to look at the biographical note about her:

> Susan Dynarski is a professor of education, public policy and economics at the University of Michigan. Follow her on Twitter: @dynarski.

This is a good sign—that the author has academic credentials on the subject she's writing about. This also means that's she likely to mention actual research on her subject matter, and that's what we want to find. Because she's writing in a newspaper, she's not going to cite her sources as you would in a paper for a class. Instead, she'll summarize the research briefly, usually giving us enough information (author name, year the research was done, etc.) to find those sources on our own. In this case, though, it's even easier because she links directly to some key articles:

> At the United States Military Academy, a <u>team of professors</u> studied laptop use in an introductory economics class. The course

> is that the learning of students seated near the laptop users was also <u>negatively affected</u>.

The sample paper in Chapter 9 uses the sources Dynarski links to, and they're both excellent. The sample paper in Chapter 8 uses Dynarski as a source.

TIP If you want to stay on the page you're reading (the Dynarski article), hold down the SHIFT key while clicking on the link—that will make the link open in a new tab.

GET ORGANIZED

It's easy to become overwhelmed with too many sources, so I recommend that you develop a system for keeping track of what you read and how to get back to it.

First, create a new document (separate from the paper, once you start writing it) just to keep source information. This is what my notes on sources looks like:

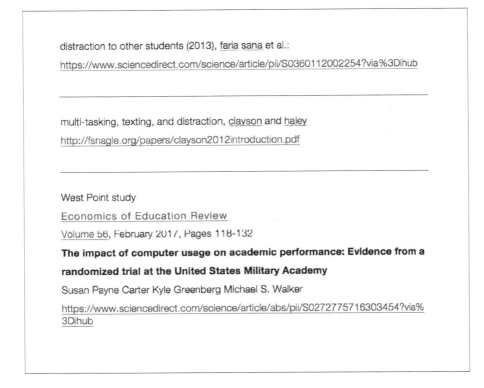

It might look a little sloppy, but who cares? The point was only for me to have a brief description of the source, simplified author information, and a link to get back to the article. I didn't need to write a description for the third source because the title makes it clear what it's about.

 TIP To get a line between each entry, type three hyphens and then hit ENTER / RETURN.

GOOGLE SCHOLAR

If your assignment requires you to find scholarly sources, Google Scholar is a very good place to begin. (Note: Google Books is similarly useful; in fact, many results you find in Scholar will be for books. You can't always read the entire book, but it's still a very good resource.) To get to Google Scholar, simply type the word *scholar* into a Google search field:

> 🔍 scholar   🎤

Once you're on the Scholar site, search as you normally would in Google—with a few exceptions you'll see on the following pages:

Google Scholar

> laptops college classroom   🔍
>
> ● Articles   ○ Case law

Most of the results were at least ten years old:

Articles	About 49,500 results (0.03 sec)
Any time Since 2020 Since 2019 Since 2016 Custom range...	**Laptops in the classroom** AB Campbell, RP Pargas - ACM SIGCSE Bulletin, 2003 - dl.acm.org ... http://www.cs.msstate.edu/ NEWS/archives/issue_1/**laptops**.html [9] MicroSoft Corporation ... windows/NetMeeting/Features/W hiteboard/ [11] Moss, W. Laptop Learning in Activities in the **Classroom**, Dept. of Mathematics, **College** of Engineering and Science, Clemson University ... ☆ ⁇ Cited by 96 Related articles All 10 versions
Sort by relevance Sort by date	**Laptops in the classroom**: do they make a difference? RL Kolar, DA Sabatini, LD Fink - Journal of Engineering ..., 2002 - Wiley Online Library ... [1] Angelo, TA, and KP Cross. 1994. **Classroom** Assessment Tech- niques: A Handbook for **College** Teachers. 2nd revised edition. San Francisco: Jossey-Bass. [2] Ayres, I. Lectures vs. **laptops**. NY Times, March 20, 2001. [3] Bloom, BS, JT Hastings, and GF Madaus. 1971 ... ☆ ⁇ Cited by 45 Related articles All 5 versions
✓ include patents ✓ include citations ✉ Create alert	Banning **Laptops** in the **Classroom**: Is it Worth the Hassles? K Yamamoto - Journal of Legal Education, 2007 - JSTOR ... 30, 2006 (**laptops** not al in certain classes in the University of Kansas Schools of Journalism and Architecture in the **College** of Liberal Arts and Sciences) . 33. See Read, A Law Professor Bans **Laptops** From the **Classroom**, supra note 29 ... ☆ ⁇ Cited by 88 Related articles All 4 versions

I knew that I wanted more recent research, so I first tried clicking on the left side of the page where it says **Since 2016**. That gave me plenty of much more recent research, but if it hadn't, I would have used the custom date range function (see page 100).

In many cases, you'll be able to go directly to the articles you want to read, but sometimes the link will take you to a site where you would have to pay to read the entire article:

I didn't intend to pay, so I did a new search with key terms from the article title and found it here:

The impact of computer usage on academic performance: Evidence from a randomized trial at the United States Military Academy
SP Carter, K Greenberg, MS Walker - Economics of Education Review, 2017 - Elsevier
... computer usage reduces academic performance among undergraduate students at a private liberal arts **college** ... the potential impact of a teacher's decision to permit or restrict **laptops** and tablets ... The United States **Military** Academy at West Point, NY, is a 4-year undergraduate ...
☆ ⟷ Cited by 89   Related articles   All 18 versions

This link took me to another paywall, so I next clicked here. On the next page, I saw 18 versions of the article, and I chose this one:

[PDF] The impact of computer usage on academic performance: Evidence from a   [PDF] army.mil
randomized trial at the United States Military Academy R
SP Carter, K Greenberg, MS Walker - oema.army.mil
abstract We present findings from a study that prohibited computer devices in randomly
selected classrooms of an introductory economics course at the United States Military
Academy. Average final exam scores among students assigned to classrooms that allowed ...
₉₉

I saw other PDF versions of the article, but I liked that this one is from the USMA, and I noticed too that it linked to a true PDF of the article as it was published, with accurate page numbers. Whenever possible, work from the PDF that gives you the actual pages from the publication.

LIBRARY DATABASES

Many professors will require that you do some or much of your research in a library database. They are incredibly powerful resources which will be increasingly useful to you as move to more advanced courses.

WHAT IS A DATABASE?

A database is a collection of articles (and other materials) from magazines, newspapers, encyclopedias, and scholarly journals. There are databases devoted to nursing, education, veterinary medicine, and many other fields. Generally, databases are available only by subscription; your college pays a considerable amount of money so that you can have access to these materials.

HOW DO YOU GET TO THE DATABASES?

Most students will get to the databases via their college library's web page, which means first going to the college homepage. From there, the method of accessing the databases will vary. Below I demonstrate how it works at my college. If your college's site is confusing, ask a librarian for directions.

Note: You'll need to log in if you're working off campus.

On the next page, you can see all the databases available to you—this is worth remembering when you need to do more advanced research in those disciplines.

For basic research, the first one, **General Databases** (**Popular**), will work well.

DATABASES & JOURNALS

General Databases (Popular)

General Databases (Scholarly)

Accounting

American Sign Language

Anthropology

Art

Astronomy

Biography

Biology

Business Administration

Career and College Resources

Chemistry

Citation Tools

Communication

Computer Science/Info Systems

Criminal Justice

Culinary Arts

Current & Controversial Issues

Deaf Studies

Developmental Disabilities

Earth Science

Economics

Education

Elections – New!

Engineering

English Composition

English Literature

English as a Second Language

Environmental Science

Fact Checking Websites (Fake News)

Forensic Science

French

Geography

Gerontology

Health

Health Information Management

Health, Fitness, Nutrition

History

Hospitality

Human Services

Information Security

Law

Management

Marketing

Mathematics

Medical Assisting

Music

Newspapers

Nursing

Nutrition

One Community Holyoke Theme

Pharmacology

Philosophy

Physics

Political Science

Psychology

Radiology

Reference Books Online

Sociology

Spanish

Speech

Sport Administration

Statistics

Sustainability

Theater

Veterinary and Animal Science

Women's Studies

CHOOSING A DATABASE AND SEARCHING

After selecting **General Databases (Popular)**, you need to choose a specific database. MasterFILE Premier should appear at or near the top, and it's the one I recommend.

> ### MASTERFILE PREMIER
> Designed specifically for public libraries, this multidisciplinary database provides full text for nearly 1,950 general reference publications with full text information dating as far back as 1975. Covering virtually every subject area of general interest, MasterFILE Premier also includes nearly 500 full text reference books, 84,011 biographies, 83,472 primary source documents, and an Image Collection of 192,999 photos, maps and flags.

Once you're in the MasterFILE Premier database, you can enter your search terms in the fields here. Remember that the databases do not typically respond well to Google-style search terms; enter just a word or two in each field:

Searching: **MasterFILE Premier** | Choose Databases

	Select a Field (optional) ▾	Search
AND ▾	Select a Field (optional) ▾	Create Alert
AND ▾	Select a Field (optional) ▾	Clear ⑦

TIP If you're researching a controversial topic, these databases are a great place to start:

> ### ISSUES & CONTROVERSIES
> Provides up-to-date, in-depth factual information on a broad range of current issues and controversies.

> ### OPPOSING VIEWPOINTS IN CONTEXT
> This database provides contextual information and opinions on hundreds of today's hottest social issues including the Death Penalty, Gun Control, Genetic Engineering, Censorship, Endangered Species, and Terrorism.

Notice that in the second field I typed the word *college*, and it suggested a number of ways to finish the term, so I chose the third one. Because it uses the word *or*, it will find articles that include any of those words.

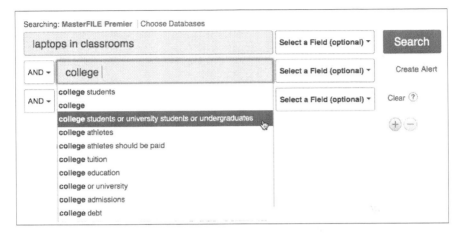

I'm skipping past the display of results for now, but I'll come back to it on page 111. After reading quickly through the first eight or ten results, one article looked promising, so I decided to look at it more closely.

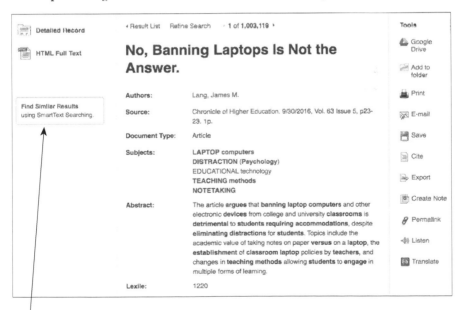

This is a very useful tool, particularly when your initial search results aren't great. I clicked on it, which led me to the excellent article on the next page.

A few features to be aware of on the article page

Doing your research in the databases has some advantages over Google Scholar, especially when it comes to keeping track of your sources and keeping them organized.

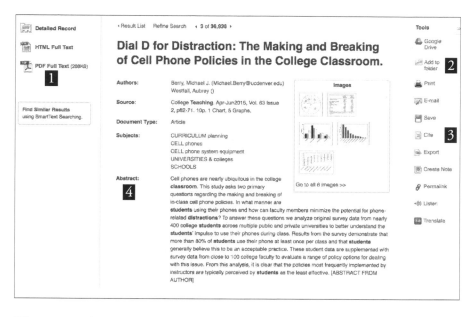

1 **PDF Full Text:** Always work from the PDF if there's one available. That way, your in-text citations will have accurate page numbers.

2 **Add to folder:** I tend to jump from one article to another quickly, and then I can't find my way back to one I knew I wanted to read. Solution: Every time you find an article you think could be useful, put it in the folder.

3 **Cite:** If you know you're going to use this article in your paper, get the citation for it now and save it in a document separate from your paper (see page 103). Remember to choose MLA or APA as your assignment calls for, and also be aware that these citations are generally correct but always need some minor fixes. See page 214 for more on using a citation generator.

4 **Abstract:** The abstract is a brief summary of the article—it's a great way to find out quickly if you want to read on.

Filtering your search results

You'll often need to filter your results, particularly by **date** (see #3 below).

1 **Full Text titles from ALL databases:** You generally want to keep both of these boxes checked—doing so will ensure that you see all the articles available for you to read.

2 **Scholarly (Peer Reviewed) Journals:** If your assignment calls for a scholarly or "peer-reviewed" article, check this box. See page 19 for more on what is meant by peer-reviewed.

3 **Publication Date:** With a current topic like the one I'm working on here, it's vital to work with the most recent research; I narrowed this one down to 2015–2020.

4 **Source Types:** When you're just getting started in your research, it's fine to see *all* results. But if you want to find higher-level research, you should check the box that limits the results to **Academic Journals**.

FINDING LIBRARY BOOKS

It may seem as if everything you could possibly need is somewhere online now, but books can be an important part of your research too.

LIBRARY

EVERYTHING | **DATABASES** | **FILMS** | **E-BOOKS** | **AUDIO**

SEARCH THE LIBRARY CATALOG

Search for:

Keyword ⬍ [1   ] [Search]

HCC Catalog | Renew Library Materials | Commonwealth Catalog

Chromebooks to borrow 2
Available now: 7 of 31
13 inch: 3 available (4 hour loan)
14 inch: 1 available (1 week loan)
15 inch: 3 available (1 week loan)

Hotspots: 13 available of 25 (1 week loan) *Coverage map*
3

OTHER RESOURCES

| **ASK A LIBRARIAN** 4 | **COURSE RESERVES** | **JOURNAL LIST** |

---

1   Enter your search terms here. As I mentioned with databases, it's smart to keep your terms simple—a couple of words rather than a long phrase.

2   Need a laptop to work on your paper? Borrow one from the library.

3   Don't have wifi at home? Borrow a hotspot.

4   Try it. You won't be sorry you did.

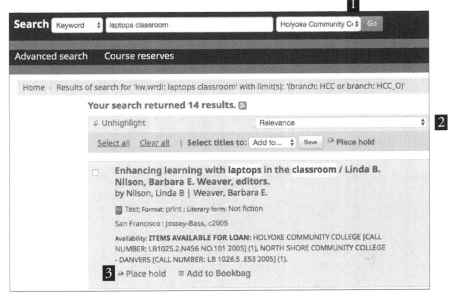

1.   Often you'll want to change this drop-down menu so that the system searches **All HELM Libraries**, or whatever larger system your college belongs to.

2.   If you want more recent books, use this drop-down menu to choose **Publication: Newest to oldest**.

3.   If you find a book you want at another library, choose **Place Hold** and enter the information to have the book sent to you at your college.

HUMANS

Go to the library and talk to a reference librarian. They enjoy working with students, and they are very talented at finding information and resources.

QD

chapter 8

MLA DOCUMENTATION

I want minimum information given with maximum politeness.
        ~ Jacqueline Kennedy

Why do your teachers care so much about documentation?

If you understand why documentation is important to academic work, you're more likely to do it accurately in your papers—and avoid a charge of plagiarism. Documenting your sources serves two purposes: First, it allows readers to know which information or ideas belong to you and which are the product of your research. Second, it enables readers to find those sources and examine them on their own.

Is this different from the documentation you learned in other courses?

Probably not. If you learned MLA documentation in high school or a previous English course, what you see in this chapter will be familiar.

When do you need to document?

You need to document your source any time you use an idea or piece of information that is not yours. If you don't document your sources properly, you may be accused of plagiarism (see page 64).

When do you *not* need to document?

You don't need to cite "common knowledge," which includes strictly factual information that can be found in a number of different sources. For example, if you were writing a paper about Ireland and wanted to mention that the Great Famine happened between 1845 and 1849, you wouldn't need to document that fact since it's widely available as a "fact" and not disputed.

MLA, APA, Chicago, etc.—which one do you use?

It depends on what kind of paper you're writing because researchers in different fields follow different rules.

In English, you use MLA (Modern Language Association), which is what this chapter covers. In psychology and other social sciences, you use APA (American Psychological Association), which I cover in Chapter 9. In history and other fields, it's the Chicago Manual of Style. For most of the sciences, it's CSE (Council of Science Editors).

All four systems have some common features, so learning MLA should help you adapt to those other documentation styles.

MLA documentation: a two-part process

Within your paper, you provide a brief reference to your source; this is called an in-text citation. At the end of the paper you provide complete information for all of your sources—this is the works-cited page.

Use the index at the end of the book

I've included many of the key search terms in the index (pages 224-229)—that's the best way to find the guideline to any documentation question you might have.

IN-TEXT CITATIONS

In all of the sample sentences below, I have *integrated* the quoted or paraphrased material into my sentences. Make sure that your sentence reads smoothly and is grammatically correct.

BASIC RULES

I'll use a recent article from *The Atlantic* about robotics in medicine for the first few examples. Note that I found this article online (theatlantic.com), though I will also go over how it would look if you use a PDF of the magazine.

Here's one part of the article that I want to use in my paper:

> Health care already represents one-sixth of America's gross domestic product. And that share is growing, placing an ever-larger strain on paychecks, corporate profits, and government resources. Figuring out how to manage this cost growth—how to meet the aging population's medical needs without bankrupting the country—has become the central economic-policy challenge of our time.

First, I put one of the ideas in my own words:

> Rising health care costs create a potential crisis for the American economy.

But this isn't my idea. *I* didn't come to this conclusion based on my research. The author of the article, Jonathan Cohn, did.

Important: No matter how you identify the "source" (usually the author), it must correspond with a works-cited entry. In other words, you must have a works-cited entry that begins Cohn, Jonathan.

Over the next few pages you can see the two basic ways to give Cohn credit, along with some complications to the basic approach.

METHOD #1: NAME THE SOURCE IN THE SENTENCE

This is the preferred method for citing a source, using the author's name in a signal phrase. (See page 57 for more information about signal phrases.)

> Jonathan Cohn argues that rising health care costs create a potential crisis for the American economy.

Note: You only write the author's full name the first time you refer to him. After that, use only the author's last name: "Cohn argues that robots. . . ."

METHOD #2: DON'T NAME THE SOURCE IN THE SENTENCE

If you don't name the source in your sentence via a signal phrase, you must do so in the parenthetical reference at the end of the sentence. Many professors prefer that students avoid this citation method; check with your professor.

> Rising health care costs create a potential crisis for the American economy (Cohn).

USING QUOTATIONS

The two methods above work the same using a *direct quotation* (the writer's exact words, in his or her order):

> Cohn observes that rising health care costs are "the central economic-policy challenge of our time."

Or:

> One commentator believes that rising health care costs are "the central economic-policy challenge of our time" (Cohn).

Note: In the first example, the period goes *inside* the quotation marks. In the second example, the period goes after the parenthetical citation. Also, be sure to type a space after closing the quotation marks.

QUOTING PART OF A SENTENCE VS. A COMPLETE SENTENCE

In most of these examples, I'm quoting part of a sentence from Cohn. See pages 59-60 for detailed information on how to quote an entire sentence correctly.

USING A SOURCE (PDF, ETC.) WITH PAGE NUMBERS

If your source is an actual book or magazine (or any other physical source with page numbers), you should include a page number in your citation. This is also the case if you're viewing a PDF that includes page numbers, which is frequently the case with scholarly articles. Here are four ways to do it:

Jonathan Cohn argues that rising health care costs create a potential crisis for the American economy (61).

Rising health care costs create a potential crisis for the American economy (Cohn 61).

Cohn observes that rising health care costs are "the central economic-policy challenge of our time" (61).

One commentator believes that rising health care costs are "the central economic-policy challenge of our time" (Cohn 61).

COMPLICATIONS TO THE BASIC RULES

Generally, the above examples will get you through the vast majority of in-text citations. But there's a good chance you'll have to deal with some variations.

TWO AUTHORS

For the sake of simplicity, let's pretend that the article in *The Atlantic* was written by Cohn and a second author, James Gillen:

> Cohn and Gillen argue that rising health care costs create a potential crisis for the American economy.

Or:

> Rising health care costs create a potential crisis for the American economy (Cohn and Gillen).

THREE OR MORE AUTHORS

If there had been a third author, you only use the first author's name, followed by **et al.** (Latin for *and others*):

> Cohn et al. argue that rising health care costs create a potential crisis for the American economy.

Or:

> Rising health care costs create a potential crisis for the American economy (Cohn et al.).

This is correct—you really do need both periods.

THREE OR MORE AUTHORS, WITH PAGE NUMBERS

> Cohn et al. argue that rising health care costs create a potential crisis for the American economy (61).

Or:

> Rising health care costs create a potential crisis for the American economy (Cohn et al. 61).

NO AUTHOR LISTED

Pretend that the article in *The Atlantic* did not have an author listed; if you use a signal phrase, provide the full title of the article (but not a subtitle):

> In "The Robot Will See You Now," the author argues that rising health care costs are "the central economic-policy challenge of our time."

If you don't use a signal phrase, shorten the article title and put it in the parenthetical citation, inside quotation marks:

> One commentator believes that rising health care costs are "the central economic-policy challenge of our time" ("Robot").

NO AUTHOR LISTED, WITH PAGE NUMBERS

> One commentator believes that rising health care costs are "the
> central economic-policy challenge of our time" ("Robot" 61).

Note: How you abbreviate the title is up to you, but be sure to use the first word that's not an article (a, an, the)—because this is the word a reader would be looking for on the works-cited page.

QUOTING SOMEONE WHO'S BEING QUOTED

This seems unusual, but it comes up often. In this example, I want to use part of the following quote, from the same article in *The Atlantic*.

> "We do now have robots performing surgery, but the robot is under constant supervision of the surgeon during the process," Baumol told a reporter from *The New York Times* two years ago. "You haven't saved labor. You have done other good things, but it isn't a way of cheapening the process."

Remember two things, and you'll get it right.

First, mention the person you're quoting (Baumol, in this case) in your sentence, and use his or her full name—which I had to find earlier in the article. Then, in your parenthetical reference, use the abbreviation *qtd. in* (for "quoted in") before the author of the article—because that's what readers will be looking for on the works-cited page if they want to find the article.

> Economist William Baumol notes that the robots are "under
> constant supervision of the surgeon during the process" (qtd. in
> Cohn).

QUOTING SOMEONE WHO'S BEING QUOTED, WITH PAGE NUMBERS

> Economist William Baumol notes that the robots are "under constant supervision of the surgeon during the process" (qtd. in Cohn 66).

CHANGING THE WORDING OF QUOTATIONS / USING BRACKETS

Generally, you should quote your sources precisely, using their exact words. But sometimes you'll need to change a word or two for grammatical purposes, or remove part of a quotation. Let's say that I want to quote part of this sentence:

> The idea of robots performing surgery or more-routine medical tasks with less supervision is something many experts take seriously.

Just for the sake of this example, let's say that I want to restructure the quoted portion of the sentence, like this:

> Cohn reports that if "robots [perform] surgery or more-routine medical tasks with less supervision," new concerns will arise.

Because I'm no longer quoting Cohn word for word (*performing* has become *perform*), I have to indicate the alteration of the original wording by putting the word I've changed inside brackets.

Note: If I chose to use the word *performed*, though, I would only put the letters I changed inside brackets:

> Cohn reports that if "robots perform[ed] surgery or more-routine medical tasks with less supervision," new concerns will arise.

LONG QUOTATION (ALSO KNOWN AS BLOCK QUOTATION)

Explanation is below; see Appendix pages 217-220 for formatting instructions.

1 By examining the marketing practices of mainstream grocery stores, Pollan reveals the preeminence of quantification:

> **2** Just look at the typical newspaper ad for a supermarket. The sole quality on display here is actually a quantity: tomatoes $0.69 a pound; ground chuck $1.09 a pound; eggs $0.99 a dozen—special this week. Is there any other category of product sold on such a reductive basis? (136) **3**

4 By highlighting the focus on price and quantity, Pollan exposes a peculiar—and potentially dangerous—complicity between consumers and grocery businesses.

1 Your writing should introduce the quotation; use the author's name in this sentence and end with a colon (:).

2 Next is the block quotation, indented an additional 1/2 inch from your left margin. Don't change the right margin. Double-space the block quotation just as you do the rest of your text. Don't use quotation marks.

3 If you're using a source with page numbers, put it at the end of the block quotation, inside parentheses, after the final punctuation mark. If you don't have a page number, do nothing.

4 Your writing after the block quotation should comment on what you just quoted.

USING ELLIPSES

If you remove a word or words from a quotation, use an ellipsis (three periods, with a space before and after each) to indicate the missing material:

> Cohn notes that if "robots [perform] surgery . . . with less supervision," new concerns will arise.

If your quotation omits material from the end of a sentence, you *may* need to use an ellipsis. The rule is this: If your quoted material forms a complete sentence, but you're not quoting the entire sentence, use an ellipsis.

> All over the country, hospitals are on a hiring binge, desperate for people who can develop and install new information systems—and then manage them or train existing workers to do so.

> Making the connection between information technology and medicine, Cohn writes, "All over the country, hospitals are on a hiring binge, desperate for people who can develop and install new information systems. . . ."

You may have noticed that I end the sentence with four periods—three periods to show the material I've removed, and one to officially end the sentence. And finally, if you're using a PDF, here's how to add the page reference in the citation:

> Cohn believes that "the efficiencies from the data revolution could amount to substantial savings. . . . That's the best reason to believe that the data revolution will make a difference . . ." (63).

WORK IN AN ANTHOLOGY

An anthology is a collection of essays, stories, or poems by many different authors. Many textbooks used in English courses are anthologies. For the in-text citation, you don't really need to worry about the fact that the book is an anthology. Just be sure that your citation refers to the actual writer of the story, poem or essay—not the editor(s) of the anthology.

> Jane Smiley suggests that the problem may have its source in "the ubiquity of sugar" (328).

Or:

> Perhaps the problem is "the ubiquity of sugar" (Smiley 328).

See page 146 for the additional information you'll need in order to do the works-cited entry.

ORGANIZATION OR GROUP AS AUTHOR

This is tricky. First, you have to determine if the author and the publisher are the same. In the case of many organizations, they will be. If you're looking at a website, you generally want to scroll down to the bottom of the screen to find the publisher's name; it's usually next to the copyright symbol.

BOTTOM OF PAGE → © 2016 Modern Language Association of America

If they're different, then simply treat the author as you normally would—you just use the organization name instead of a person's name. If the author and publisher *are* the same, you don't refer to an author in your sentence; instead, you use the title of whatever the organization wrote:

> "Foreign Languages and Higher Education: New Structures for a Changed World" reports that language schools have found it difficult to set new priorities and create new programs.

I don't think that reads well, mainly because the title of the publication is so long. In a case like this, you'd be better off referencing the source (the shortened version of the title is correct) at the end of your sentence:

> As a result of various global conflicts, language schools have found it difficult to set new priorities and create new programs ("Foreign Languages").

Note: I did not include a page number for either citation because I found the quotation on the organization's website.

AUTHOR WHO WROTE TWO OR MORE BOOKS (THAT YOU CITE IN YOUR PAPER)

Let's say that I read two books by Michael Pollan (*The Omnivore's Dilemma* and *In Defense of Food*), and I'm using them both as sources in my paper. So that there's no confusion about which book I'm referring to, I need to provide a shortened reference to the book inside the parentheses.

> Michael Pollan asserts that both our civilization and our food system are "organized on industrial lines" (*Omnivore* 201).

Or:

> It has been argued that both our civilization and our food system are "organized on industrial lines" (Pollan, *Omnivore* 201).

Note: If I had been using an article rather than a book, I would have still used a shortened form of the title, but it would be inside quotation marks, not italicized.

TWO AUTHORS WITH SAME LAST NAME

It doesn't happen very often, but it does happen. If you refer to the author within the sentence, use the first and last name each time.

> Christopher Alexander argues that a "complex of buildings with no center is like a man without a head" (486).

Or:

> One theorist asserts that "a complex of buildings with no center is like a man without a head" (C. Alexander 486).

TWO OR MORE AUTHORS IN THE SAME SENTENCE

Put the parenthetical citation immediately after the information you're citing from each author.

> It has been said that heightened awareness of the sources of our food connects people to their "agricultural roots" (Smiley 437), or even to their "feral past" (Winckler 28).

TWO AUTHORS WHO MAKE THE SAME POINT

Again, this will happen only rarely. Your citation should name both authors, separated by a semi-colon.

> America's reliance on industrial farming will have serious economic consequences that could lead to significantly more expensive food in the near future (Pollan 486; Jones 54).

CITING A KINDLE, NOOK, OR OTHER E-READER

If you were reading a physical book, you would cite the page number that you're quoting from. But because e-readers don't consistently have the same page numbering, you should *not* provide this information. Also, don't provide any other marker or indicator of location provided by the e-reader. However, if the book is divided into chapters (and you're confident that these would be the same in the physical book and in electronic versions), then do give the chapter.

> Michael Pollan asserts that both our civilization and our food system are "strictly organized on industrial lines" (ch. 10).

Or:

> In Chapter 10, "Grass," Michael Pollan asserts that both our civilization and our food system are "strictly organized on industrial lines."

RADIO PROGRAM / PODCAST / TRANSCRIPT

Treat these as you would any other source with an author. In this example, I listened to a podcast on NPR about companies sharing our online information. The author was listed as Brian Naylor.

> Brian Naylor asserts that large companies "know more about you than you can imagine."

Or, you may want to name the source—National Public Radio—specifically because it is widely viewed as a reliable source.

> According to a National Public Radio report, large companies "know more about you than you can imagine" (Naylor).

WORKS-CITED ENTRIES

FIRST, A FEW UNIVERSAL GUIDELINES

The information on the next two pages is essential—don't skip past it. And a piece of advice as you're getting started: There's not always a single right way to document a source, and sometimes you have to use some judgment.

USING A CITATION GENERATOR

Services like EasyBib, Citation Generator, and NoodleTools are great at helping you create properly formatted citations—but only if you give them the right information. Also, be aware that the citations generated in databases almost always contain errors (particularly with capitalization). See page 215-216 for more.

CAPITALIZATION

It doesn't make much sense that you're supposed to capitalize titles "properly" when the journal or magazine article you're citing hasn't done so, but that's just how it is. Even if your source doesn't capitalize properly, you need to.

So, even though a *Sports Illustrated* article appears as "Over The Top" in the database, you follow the rule that says not to capitalize articles ("the") and write the title as "Over the Top."

Always capitalize   the first and last words of the title
nouns, verbs, adjectives, and adverbs

Do *not* capitalize   prepositions: of, on, around, behind, and many more
articles: a, an, the
conjunctions: and, but, or, for, nor, so, yet
infinitive: to

URLS

When citing a URL (web address), remove http:// or https://.

LONG TITLES

Sometimes, particularly with newspaper and magazine articles, you'll come across some very long titles. Or at least they look that way; in many cases, what you're seeing is a headline and a sub-headline, as in this magazine article:

In these cases, you only want to include the first part of the title. Often, the sub-headline will be a complete sentence, and that's a good indication that it's not really part of the title. See page 133 for another example.

By contrast, if you're reading a scholarly article, the subtitle will almost always be included as part of your citation, after a colon. See page 135 for an example.

AUTHOR NAMES

The basic rule is that you reverse the order of the first author's name, but leave the others in the usual order.

One author: Smith, Doug K.

> If Smith didn't have a middle initial: Smith, Doug.

Two authors: Smith, Doug K., and Walter T. White.

> If Smith didn't have a middle initial: Smith, Doug, and Walter T. White.

Three or more authors: Smith, Doug K., et al.

> If Smith didn't have a middle initial: Smith, Doug, et al.

(Et al. is an abbreviation for *and others*.)

ABBREVIATIONS OF MONTHS

Most months are abbreviated; here's how all of them should look:

Jan.	Feb.	Mar.	Apr.
May	June	July	Aug.
Sept.	Oct.	Nov.	Dec.

ABBREVIATION OF PUBLISHERS' NAMES

If the publisher is listed as, for example, The Macmillan Company, you would simply write Macmillan. For academic journals, the publisher is often a university press. If, for example, it's Harvard University Press, you would abbreviate it Harvard UP or, for the University of Chicago Press, it would be U of Chicago P (no period—but my sentence now needs one).

SPACES

With some of the examples on the following pages, it's hard to tell where you should have a space. You always have a space after any mark of punctuation (comma, period, colon, semi-colon); also remememuber that between each "part" of an entry (like, for example, between a magazine name and its date of publication), you always need a space. The only exception to this rule is when you're using quotation marks, which come immediately after a comma or period, like "this," or "this."

HANGING INDENT

One of the unusual characteristics of the works-cited page is the "hanging indent." We do it this way because the Modern Language Association tells us to, but also because it makes sense. When you have quite a few works-cited entries, it's easier for the reader to find a particular source by browsing down the left side of the page (where all entries are alphabetized) to find the author name. See pages 219-221 for how to do it the right way—don't use the TAB key.

PAGE RANGES

If you're writing page numbers over 100, write them like this: 113-16 (*not* 113-116) or 1062-65 (*not* 1062-1065).

INTERNET AND DATABASE SOURCES

ARTICLE YOU FOUND ONLINE

This is the guideline you'd use for just about any "article" you find online.

Author's Last Name, First Name. "Title of Article: Subtitle." *Name of website*, date, URL. Date accessed.

Cohn, Jonathan. "The Robot Will See You Now." *The Atlantic*, 20 Feb. 2013, www.theatlantic.com/magazine/archive/2013/03/the-robot-will-see-you/309216. Accessed 12 Mar. 2020.

Generally, you should not include subtitles for magazine articles (see guidelines for long titles on page 130).

ARTICLE YOU FOUND ONLINE, WITH COMPLICATIONS

This is the same guideline as on the previous page, but it has some additional elements that make it slightly more complicated.

This is an unusual title for two reasons: First, you need quotation marks around the first two words, which means you need to use single quotation marks, 'like this,' around those words. But your entire title needs to have standard quotation marks, "like this."

Second, the title includes a period and a second "sentence." It's not exactly a sentence, but it's definitely part of the title—and not a subtitle. In many cases, though, you would not want to include an additional sentence that appears after the title. See more about long titles on page 130. One lesson: Sometimes you have to make some judgment calls.

Author's Last Name, First Name. "Title of Article: Subtitle." Name

of website, date, URL. Date accessed.

Quart, Alissa. "'Middle Class' Used to Denote Comfort and

Security. Not Anymore." *The Guardian*, 7 July 2016, www.

theguardian.com/commentisfree/2016/jul/07/middle-class-

struggle-technology-overtaking-jobs-security-cost-of-living.

Accessed 6 Feb. 2020.

ARTICLE IN A DATABASE

This is the same article from two pages back; I'm going over it again so you can see how the citation is slightly different when you find the article in a database rather than as a result of a regular internet search.

NAME OF DATABASE

Searching: **MasterFILE Premier** | Choose Databases

EBSCOhost

robot will see you now

Select a Field (optional) ▾

◻ Detailed Record ◻ HTML Full Text ◻ PDF Full Text (9.6MB)

PDF

‹ Result List   Refine Search   ‹ 1 of 4 ›   **ARTICLE TITLE**

THE ROBOT WILL SEE YOU NOW. (cover story)

Authors: COHN, JONATHAN () — **AUTHOR**

Source: Atlantic. Mar2013, Vol. 311 Issue 2, p58-67. 9p. 4 Color Photographs.

KEY PUBLICATION INFO

Author's Last Name, First Name. "Title of Article: Subtitle." *Name of Publication*, vol. X, no. X, date, page range. *Name of Database*, URL or DOI. Date accessed.

Cohn, Jonathan. "The Robot Will See You Now." *The Atlantic*, vol. 311, no. 2, Mar. 2013, pp. 58-69. *MasterFILE Premier*, web.a.ebscohost.com.ezproxyhcc.helmlib.org/ehost/detail/detail?vid=6&sid=25253&db=f5h. Accessed 16 Jan. 2020.

A few things to notice about how you write the title:

• not in all caps   • don't include "(cover story)"   • no extra period after Now

Also, most magazines won't have volume and issue information, so you ordinarily you wouldn't include that; but it's here, so we'll add it. Finally, always use the PDF option when you have it (see page 110).

ARTICLE (SCHOLARLY) IN A DATABASE OR ONLINE

Use the guideline below if you find a scholarly article in a database. If you find it online, simply remove the name of the database.

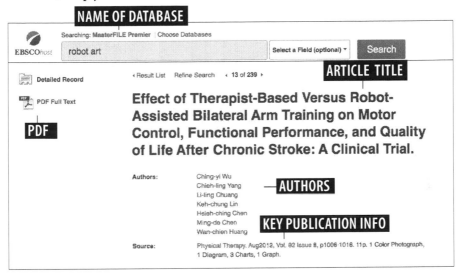

Author's Last Name, First Name. "Title of Article: Subtitle." *Name of Publication*, vol. X, no. X, date, page range. *Name of Database*, URL or DOI. Date accessed.

Wu, Ching-yi, et al. "Effect of Therapist-Based Versus Robot-Assisted Bilateral Arm Training on Motor Control, Functional Performance, and Quality of Life after Chronic Stroke: A Clinical Trial." *Physical Therapy*, vol. 92, no. 8, Aug. 2012, pp. 1006-16. *MasterFILE Premier*, doi.org/10.2522/ptj.20110282. Accessed 16 Jan. 2020.

Always look for the DOI (digital object identifier); I found it after the abstract. Also note that the page numbers are *not* written as 1006-1016.

BLOG POST

You'll notice that this is almost exactly like the format for any online article. The only real difference is that on many blogs, writers don't use their full names—or they use a pseudonym. Whatever name the person uses is the one you should use for your works-cited entry.

NAME OF WEBSITE

WATCHERS ON THE WALL

A Game of Thrones Community for Breaking News, Casting, and Commentary

Unity and nihilism in Game of Thrones and A Song of Ice and Fire — **BLOG POST TITLE**

Posted on July 11, 2016 by Petra — **AUTHOR**

DATE OF PUBLICATION

Note that I added italics to the titles of the TV show and the book. It's the same principle that tells us to fix the capitalization of titles.

Author. "Title of Blog Post." *Name of website*, date, URL. Date

accessed.

Petra. "Unity and Nihilism in *Game of Thrones* and *A Song of Ice and Fire*." *Watchers on the Wall*, 11 July 2016, watchersonthewall. com/unity-nihilism-game-thrones-song-ice-fire/. Accessed 2 July 2019.

Note: The blog post title is unusual because it's inside quotation marks—but I do need to italicize the titles of the movie and the book there too.

DOCUMENT PUBLISHED BY GOVERNMENT AGENCY

If you're using an entire publication, as in the case below, this is the appropriate guideline. If you're using a web page published by an organization (including a government organization), use the guideline on the next page.

Start by providing the name of the government—in the U.S., this will typically be either United States or the name of a state—followed by the name of the agency that published the document. You may also need to list a "sub-agency." Note: I found the reference to the Department of Education at the bottom of the page.

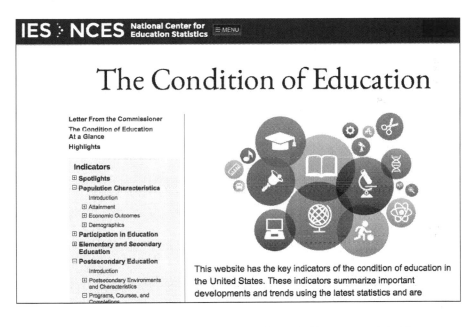

Government, Agency, Sub-Agency [if needed]. *Name of Publication*,

date, URL. Date accessed.

United States, Department of Education, National Center for

Education Statistics. *The Condition of Education*, 2016, nces.

ed.gov/programs/coe/. Accessed 23 Aug. 2019.

ONLINE PAGE PUBLISHED BY GOVERNMENT AGENCY OR AN ORGANIZATION

In many cases, the author is the same as the publisher. When that's the case, you don't list an author—go straight to the title of the article.

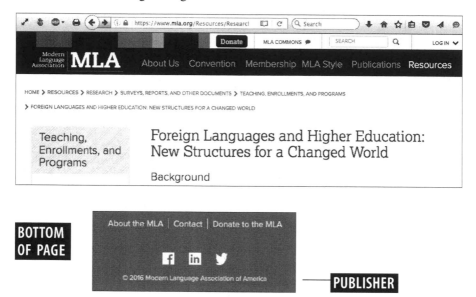

"Title of Article." *Name of website*, publisher, date, URL. Date

accessed.

"Foreign Languages and Higher Education: New Structures for a

Changed World." *MLA*, Modern Language Association of

America, www.mla.org/Resources/Research/Surveys-Reports/

Foreign-Languages-and-Higher-Education-New-Structures-

for-a-Changed-World. Accessed 6 July 2019.

I didn't include a date in my entry because there was none listed. If the article does include a date, put it after the publisher, before the URL.

ARTICLE WITH NO AUTHOR

As with many "news" stories online, there's no author listed for this article. Start with the article title and proceed as you would with other online entries: name of webpage, date, URL. Date accessed.

"911 Caller: Husband Won't Eat Dinner." *NBC News*, 24 Dec.

2009, www.nbcnews.com/id/34577354/ns/us_news-weird_

news/t/caller-husband-wont-eat-dinner/#.V4UcCa7flUM.

Accessed 23 Aug. 2019.

TWITTER

Start with the writer's screen name, followed by actual name (if provided) in parentheses, followed by the entire Tweet, inside quotation marks—you *don't* need to correct the capitalization—but do capitalize the first word. Include hashtags if they're part of the Tweet.

@eyeballhatred (Clay Banes). "Life is like a tree / in the men's room

/ at Auto Express in Hadley, MA. @ Auto Express Hadley."

25 June 2016, 10:02 a.m. *Twitter*, twitter.com/eyeballhatred/

status/7467593856. Accessed 23 Aug. 2019.

PODCAST / RADIO PROGRAM

Let's say that you heard a program on NPR (National Public Radio) that you want to use in your paper. If you can't find an author's name, start your entry with the title of the podcast.

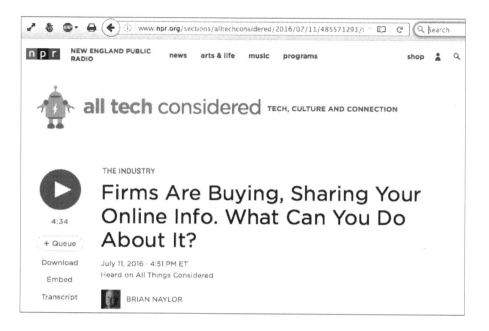

Author's Last Name, First Name. "Title of Podcast / Article." *Name of website*, date, URL. Transcript. Date accessed.

Naylor, Brian. "Firms Are Buying, Sharing Your Online Info. What Can You Do About It?" *National Public Radio*, 11 July 2016, www.npr.org/sections/alltechconsidered/2016/07/11/485571291/firms-are-buying-sharing. Transcript. Accessed 23 Aug. 2019.

YOUTUBE / VIMEO / ONLINE VIDEO

These are generally like online articles.

Author Last Name, First Name. "Title of Video: Subtitle." *Name of website*, date, URL. Date accessed.

Spokane Public Schools. "What Do You Do? Occupational Therapist." *YouTube*, 5 May 2017, www.youtube.com/watch?v=WJs7dge75uM. Accessed 16 Feb. 2019.

Remeber: Fix the capitalization in the title as needed and remove http:// from the URL.

ONLINE VIDEO / TEDTALK

Because TED is considered a publisher, you should add some information to your entry. The other element that can be confusing is that the author's name is generally listed with the title.

Author Last Name, First Name. "Title of Video: Subtitle." *Name of Organization Hosting the Talk / Video*, date of publication. *Name of website*, URL. Date accessed.

Scott, Sophie. "Why We Laugh." *TED*, 3 Apr. 2012. *YouTube*, www.youtube.com/watch?v=UxLRv0FEndM&list=PL70DE C2B0568B5469&index=22. Accessed 23 Feb. 2020.

BOOKS

Where to find key publication information:

- Title, subtitle, and author name will be on the cover of the book, obviously, though sometimes the formatting is unusual, in which case you're better off looking at the title page.

- The title page is usually the first "real" page of the book, or soon after. The publisher's name is almost always there. The spine of the book usually has the publisher's name too.

- The year of publication will be on the copyright page, after the © symbol.

BOOK WITH ONE AUTHOR

Author's Last Name, First Name. *Book Title: Book Subtitle**.

Publisher, Year of Publication.

* Include subtitle after a colon, and always capitalize the first word after the colon.

Pollan, Michael. *The Omnivore's Dilemma: A Natural History of Four Meals*. Penguin, 2006.

BOOK WITH TWO, THREE, OR MORE AUTHORS

See guidelines on page 130 for how to write additional author names.

BOOK WITH AN EDITOR

The editor is listed as the "main" author for the sake of the works-cited entry. Keep in mind, though, that if you cite particular essays or stories from within this book, you need an entry for each of these authors too. Yes, this is a little confusing. See also the guideline for *Work(s) in an anthology* on page 146-147.

As far as the works-cited entry goes, this is just like any other book, with the simple addition of the word *editor(s)*.

> Hofstadter, Albert, and Richard Kuhns, editors. *Philosophies of*
>
> *Art and Beauty: Selected Readings in Aesthetics from Plato to*
>
> *Heidegger*. U of Chicago P, 1964.

BOOK THAT LISTS AN EDITION

Many books (textbooks, especially) are republished with the same title but new content. If your book has an edition listed, it will probably be noticeable on the cover and/or the spine. In the works-cited entry, put the edition after the title.

> McQuade, Donald, and Robert Atwan, editors. *The Writer's Presence:*
>
> *A Pool of Readings*. 9th ed., Bedford / St. Martin's, 2018.

KINDLE, NOOK, IPAD, OR E-BOOK

If you read the book on a Kindle, Nook, iPad, or similar device, you don't need to add anything to your entry.

However, if you read an e-book online, you should include information about the name of the site where you viewed it (an app called OverDrive, in this case), italicized, and the URL, if available:

> Shteyngart, Gary. *Super Sad True Love Story*. Random House, 2010.
>
> *OverDrive*, ofs-650f28f6a35e6f81781172bfd6f72d78.read.
>
> overdrive.com/?p=PKb5Agh1yKwg. Accessed 19 Mar. 2020.

BOOK BY AN ORGANIZATION OR GROUP

If the author and the publisher are the same, start with the book title.

MLA Style Manual and Guide to Scholarly Publishing. 8th ed.,

Modern Language Association of America, 2016.

TWO OR MORE BOOKS BY SAME AUTHOR

Use three hyphens to indicate a repeat of the author's name. Put each book in alphabetical order (*In* before *Omnivore*).

Pollan, Michael. *In Defense of Food: An Eater's Manifesto.* Penguin,

2008.

---. *The Omnivore's Dilemma: A Natural History of Four Meals.*

Penguin, 2006.

BOOK BY AN ANONYMOUS AUTHOR

Don't write Anonymous or Anon. for the author. Just go straight to the title.

Primary Colors: A Novel of Politics. Random House, 2006.

BOOK THAT HAS BEEN TRANSLATED

Start with the person who wrote the book, *not* the translator.

Barthes, Roland. *The Eiffel Tower and Other Mythologies.* Translated

by Richard Howard, Noonday, 1979.

BOOK IN MORE THAN ONE VOLUME

After the title, write the volume number that you used.

> Kelby, Scott. *The Digital Photography Book*. Vol. 2, Peachpit Press,
>
> 2008.

BOOK THAT HAS A TITLE WITHIN THE TITLE

When scholars write about another book, they often include the title of the book in *their* title. Don't italicize the title that appears within their title.

> Brodhead, Richard H., editor. *New Essays on* Moby-Dick.
>
> Cambridge UP, 1986.

WORK IN AN ANTHOLOGY—A BOOK WITH MANY DIFFERENT AUTHORS

An anthology is a collection of works (essays, stories, poems, and/or plays) written by many different authors. If you're using one essay from an anthology, here's how you cite it:

Author's Last Name, First Name. "Title of Essay." *Name of Book*,

edited by First Name Last Name, edition, Publisher, Year of

Publication, page range.

> Hughes, Langston. "Salvation." *The Writer's Presence: A Pool of*
>
> *Readings*, edited by Donald McQuade and Robert Atwan, 5th
>
> ed., Bedford / St. Martin's, 2007, pp. 163-65.

- This is the guideline for when you're citing only one essay, story, play, or poem from an anthology; if you cite more than one, see the next entry.
- The editors' names will be on the front of the book and on the title page.

TWO OR MORE WORKS FROM THE SAME ANTHOLOGY

When you use two different authors from the same anthology, you use what the MLA calls a "cross-reference." Do a shortened entry for each essay, story, or poem, and also do a full entry for the whole book.

Note: Put each entry on your works-cited page wherever it belongs alphabetically; in other words, these would not necessarily be grouped together.

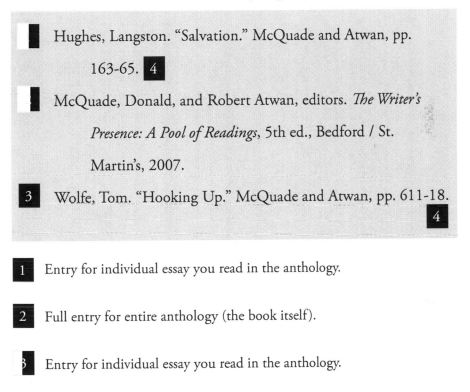

Hughes, Langston. "Salvation." McQuade and Atwan, pp. 163-65. **4**

McQuade, Donald, and Robert Atwan, editors. *The Writer's Presence: A Pool of Readings*, 5th ed., Bedford / St. Martin's, 2007.

3 Wolfe, Tom. "Hooking Up." McQuade and Atwan, pp. 611-18. **4**

1 Entry for individual essay you read in the anthology.

2 Full entry for entire anthology (the book itself).

3 Entry for individual essay you read in the anthology.

Note that when you have a range of pages over 100, this is the correct way to write them. It should *not* be 163-165 or 611-618.

WORK IN A PROFESSOR'S "COURSE PACKET" OR HANDOUT

Ideally, your professor has provided citation information for the source, in which case you should use his or her citation. If not, start with the author and title of the work you're citing, followed by the most logical information about the course packet you can find. If the professor has titled the course packet, use that as the title and name him/her as the person who "compiled" the selections, followed by information about the course.

Author's Last Name, First Name. "Title of Essay." *Title of Course*

   Packet, compiled by First Name Last Name, course handout,

   Name of Course and Course Number, Name of College,

   Semester and Year, page range.

Saunders, George. "Escape from Spiderhead." *The Persistence of*

   Reality: Readings, compiled by James Dutcher, course handout,

   English 230, Holyoke Community College, Fall 2018, pp.

   163-65.

If the course packet has no title, use this guideline:

Saunders, George. "Escape from Spiderhead." Course handout,

   compiled by James Dutcher, English 230, Holyoke

   Community College, Fall 2018, pp. 163-65.

GRAPHIC NOVEL OR COMIC BOOK

For a comic book, you should identify the title of the particular issue you're using, followed by the title of the series.

Author's Last Name, First Name. *Title of Issue*. *Title of Series*, issue

number, Publisher, Year of Publication.

Lemire, Jeff. *Machine Moon*. *Descender*, no. 2, Image Comics, 2016.

ENCYCLOPEDIA OR DICTIONARY

In most reference books (such as encyclopedias and dictionaries), no author is listed, so you simply start with the title of the entry. After the name of the book, include the edition (abbreviated as below) and the year. If there *is* an author listed, then put that first. But I have a feeling you knew that.

"Botox." *The New Encyclopædia Britannica*. 15th ed. 2003.

If you use an online encyclopedia, see the next guideline for an online book.

BOOK THAT YOU READ ONLINE

Author's Last Name, First Name. *Book Title: Book Subtitle*. Publisher,

Year of Publication. *Name of Site*, URL. Date accessed.

Orejan, Jaime. *Football / Soccer: History and Tactics*. McFarland,

2011. *Google Books*, books.Google.com/books?id=H0l2T7tLS

iEC&lpg=PP1&dq=soccer%20football&pg=PR4#v=onepage

&q=soccer%20football&f=false. Accessed 12 May 2019.

OTHER SOURCES

FILM / DVD (OF A MOVIE, NOT A TV SHOW)

Title of Film. Directed by First Name Last Name, Name of Studio that produced film, Year of release.

Inglourious Basterds. Directed by Quentin Tarantino, Universal Pictures, 2009.

TELEVISION SHOW

"Title of Episode." *Title of Show*, created by First Name Last Name, season X, episode X, *Publisher*, date show aired or was released. *Site where you viewed episode*, URL.

"Buckle Up." *Scandal*, created by Shonda Rhimes, season 5, episode 19, *ABC*, 28 Apr. 2016. *Hulu*, www.hulu.com/watch/935545.

If you watched it on TV rather than streaming, eliminate the last two elements (*Hulu* and the URL).

INTERVIEW

Last Name, First Name (of person you interviewed). Personal interview, date of interview.

Gillen, Claire. Personal interview, 29 June 2019.

E-MAIL MESSAGE

Last Name, First Name (of person who wrote email). "Subject of
Message." Received by Your Name (or name of person who
received the message, if not you), date of e-mail.

Van Duren, Marsha. "Re: Further Thoughts on Writing Process."
Received by Fred Cooksey, 25 Feb. 2020.

IMAGE / PHOTOGRAPH / ARTWORK

If you viewed the artwork in person rather than online, don't include the name
of the website or the URL.

Artist's Last Name, First Name. *Title of artwork.* Year the artwork
was produced, Museum or Gallery where it is found, City of
Museum/Gallery. *Name of website*, URL.

Giacometti, Alberto. *Man Pointing.* 1947, Tate Gallery, London.
Tate, www.tate.org.uk/art/artworks/giacometti-man-
pointing-n05939.

If the artwork does not appear to be part of a museum or gallery collection—if,
for example, it only exists online—then format it like a standard web page.

Name of artist. "Title of artwork." *Website name*, year the artwork
was produced, URL. Date accessed.

Thayer, Tim. "Robot England." *OtterJet*, 2015, otterjet.com/works/
robot-england/. Accessed 20 Jan. 2020.

SAMPLE PAPER (MLA)

I put the name "Roger Hughes" on this paper, but I wrote it—not because I haven't received excellent student papers, but because I wanted to demonstrate some specific techniques. I also wanted you to see how this paper compares to the one at the end of the next chapter (which I also wrote) since they share a number of sources and strategies. An outline for this paper appears on page 76.

You might also be interested to know that I thought I could write these papers in about two or three hours (each). Including time for finding, reading, and making some notes on the source material, I think it took me closer to eight hours to write the first one. The second one was a little quicker, but only because I was using a number of the same sources. Writing comes pretty easily to me, but this work wasn't as easy as I thought it was going to be.

And in case you're interested, this paper doesn't reflect what I think about this subject. But it is a fascinating exercise to write an essay from a perspective or position that you don't actually hold. (Law schools force students to do exactly this as part of their training.)

FORMATTING GUIDELINES

See Appendix (pages 214-223) for instructions on formatting in Google Docs and Microsoft Word.

Margins: 1 inch on all sides. Indent all paragraphs 1/2 inch.

Spacing: Double-space everything, including the works-cited page.

SPECIFIC FORMATTING ELEMENTS *(see facing page for number references)*

1   Your last name and page number should appear on every page.

2   Your name and class information should appear in the order shown here. Double-space this information just as you do the rest of the paper.

3   Title: Don't use bold, italics or underlining. See page 51 for additional guidelines.

1 Hughes 1

2 Roger Hughes

Professor Cooksey

English 101.15

6 December 2019

3 Let the Students Type (and Text, and Shop):

College Classrooms Need to Embrace Student Use of Technology

More than 2500 years ago, the Greek philosopher Socrates 4

had nothing good to say about people—like his student Plato—

who wanted to write down their discussions of reality, ethics, and

government. Socrates thought that if people couldn't hold all the

ideas in their heads, then they didn't really "know" those ideas.

It seems absurd now, but how different is it in 2020 when many

professors tell students they can't use a laptop to take notes? These

professors argue that a complete prohibition is necessary both for

their own focus while teaching and for the protection of students

who might be distracted by their peers' use of phones and laptops.

Other faculty take a more relaxed approach, in some cases because

they have given up trying to enforce stricter policies, but also

because they truly believe in the benefits of students having access

---

4 Let's imagine that "Roger" had recently taken a philosophy class and remembered this information about Socrates and Plato. Tip: Use what you learn in other classes to help give broader context to your introduction (and possibly the conclusion too).

Hughes 2

to a variety of technological tools in the classroom. In spite of some   5
potential challenges, both students and professors would benefit
from allowing more rather than less technology in the classroom.

One argument for more relaxed electronics policies is that   6
students should have the right—within reason—to use whatever
tools they need in order to learn most effectively. Put another way,
why should any individual professor have the right to control how
a student chooses to master the course material? Students are the
ones paying for the course, and if they feel that they can perform
at a higher level with the assistance of a laptop or tablet, then they
should not be barred from using those devices. Susan Dynarski, a
professor at the University of Michigan, notes that "most college
students are legal adults who can serve in the armed forces, vote
and own property." In other words, college students have significant
and important rights outside of the classroom, so they should not
have to give up such a basic one in the classroom.

5   Your thesis statement should generally be the last sentence of your
introduction.

6   Every body paragraph should start with a topic sentence that clearly states
what the paragraph will be concerned with. See page 77.

Hughes 3

This concept of student rights extends to the use of other, supposedly distracting, devices—like phones for texting. For many students, sending and receiving texts is one way to be available if they are needed in an emergency. Preventing them from receiving a text in such a situation simply because it violates the professor's "policy" seems overly controlling and potentially unethical. Additionally, some students perceive texting as a way to aid their focus during class, arguing that it is "just like . . . doodling" and that it "helps me listen better" (Williams et al. 54). If students feel that these devices are helpful in their learning, they should have the right to take advantage of them.

Of course, every student and professor knows that most students are on their phones and laptops for reasons that have nothing to do with being available for possible emergencies or improving their concentration. They use them because they're bored—so isn't it fair for professors to try to prevent students from engaging in these counterproductive behaviors? Many students would say no, arguing that because many college lectures are

7

7 Here the paper introduces a naysayer (see page 80). It also makes a transition from the previous paragraph by reusing those details about emergencies and concentration, but for a new purpose—to give the reader a different way of thinking about student rights.

Hughes 4

unengaging, students should be free to do what they like during class, particularly if they are not disturbing other students. Students have justified texting during class, for example, by saying, "I'm not learning anyway" and "I text because I'm bored, so I was not learning to begin with" (Williams et al. 54-55). Rather than faulting students for being bored during class, professors should reexamine their teaching methods. Beyond this, too, it may be the case that texting is less harmful than many might think. In one study, researchers found that students' overall GPA was unaffected by their texting, concluding that "being distracting in class may not be that much of a problem" (Clayson and Haley 36). **8**

For many professors, though, the key issue is that one **9** student's use of a device can be distracting to *other students*. Sana et al. reported that students "in view of multitasking peers scored significantly lower on the test than [those] not in view of multitasking peers" (29). In other words, students did worse on **10**

---

8 Many professors don't want you to end a paragraph with a quotation. It's not ideal here, but at least it makes a good connection to the next paragraph.

9 The transitional word *though* helps the reader know that we're reversing direction from the previous paragraph; now the focus will be on how devices can distract other students.

10 Using *In other words* is a good way to force yourself to explain the quotation.

Hughes 5

tests when they could see another student who was distracted. A

student in another study put it succinctly: "I get distracted by them

being distracted" (Williams et al. 53). Some professors solve this

problem by requiring that students using laptops sit in the back

row of the classroom; other professors require students to sign a

pledge promising not to use a device for non-class activities. It is

unclear how effective either of these approaches is.

    A better solution is one that also addresses the issue of

students with disabilities. By law, professors must allow students

with documented disabilities certain "accommodations," and one   **11**

of the most common is a laptop for note-taking. If a professor

has a ban on laptops in the classroom but one student is clearly

using one, then other students in the classroom will know that

that student has a disability. This is an unacceptable and unethical

breach of that student's right to privacy. One professor, however,

has a clever and seemingly effective solution to this problem;

11 This information about the law regarding accommodations for students with disabilities doesn't need to be cited because it is both factual and available in multiple sources.

Hughes 6

Zachary Nowak banned laptops in his classroom, but made two

exceptions to the ban: 12

> Anyone who had an accommodation could use one, as could   13
>
> anyone who came to my office hours and made a case for why
>
> they wanted to use one during class. I expected a number of
>
> students to select the second option and decided I would set
>
> a relatively low bar but would ask those students to sign a
>
> contract that outlined how they would use the laptops during
>
> class.

The result was that no students requested to use a laptop, thus   14

protecting the privacy of the students with disabilities who did

use them. Nowak describes the resulting classroom atmosphere as

"palpably less distracted."

---

12 This is the beginning of a block quotation; using a colon isn't the only way to do it, but it is the most common. Formatting: See Appendix pages 217-220.

13 When your quotation is four lines or longer, you should use a block quote. The entire block quote is indented 1/2 inch from the left margin; the right margin stays the same. The first line of the block quote is never indented.

14 Because this sentence continues the ideas of the paragraph before the block quote, it isn't indented. This is where you should explain and/or comment on the information in the block quote.

Hughes 7

Nowak's approach is one that more professors should emulate.   15
Perhaps, though, the struggle against distraction is one that we
will eventually master—just as humans have mastered previous
technologies that some feared would lead to our demise. Humans
have always grappled with technological change—the written
word itself was a "technology." In other words, humans are always
adapting to new ways of exchanging and generating information in
order to make sense of the world. Today's college professors should
remember that the various devices students bring to the classroom
are merely new tools for learning—fifty years from now it will seem
quaint that we once questioned their place in college classrooms.

15   Notice that there are no sources in this final paragraph, which is appropriate.
You want to make sure that *yours* is the dominant voice in the conclusion.
One source, making a general comment that you respond to, would be
fine—but no more than that.

The concluding sentences make clear the author's voice and view on the
subject, but these are not merely a restatement of the introduction; instead, I've
put the controversy discussed in the paper in a larger context. This is effective
too because it recalls the larger ideas brought up in the introduction—that
change is necessary.

Hughes 8

Works Cited

Clayson, Dennis E., and Debra A. Haley. "An Introduction to Multitasking and Texting Prevalence and Impact on Grades and GPA in Marketing Classes." *Journal of Marketing Education.* vol. 35, no. 1, Apr. 2013, pp. 26-40. doi. org/10.1177/0273475312467339. Accessed 2 Dec. 2019.

Dynarski, Susan. "Laptops Are Great. But Not During a Lecture or a Meeting." *New York Times*, 22 Nov. 2017. www.nytimes. com/2017/11/22/business/laptops-not-during-lecture-or-meeting. html. Accessed 4 Dec. 2019.

Nowak, Zachary. "A Truce in the Laptop Wars." *Inside Higher Ed*, 12 Nov. 2019. www.insidehighered.com/advice/2019/11/12/ professor-describes-fruitful-compromise-allowing-laptop-use-class-opinion. Accessed 4 Dec. 2019.

Sana, Faria, et al. "Laptop Multitasking Hinders Classroom Learning for Both Users and Nearby Peers." *Computers & Education*, vol. 62, Mar. 2013, pp. 24-31. doi.org/10.1016/j. compedu.2012.10.003. Accessed 1 Dec. 2019.

Williams, Joan A., et al. "'I Get Distracted By Their Being Distracted': The Etiquette of In-Class Texting." *Eastern Educational Journal*, vol. 40, no. 1, Spring 2011, pp. 48-56. castle.eiu.edu/edjournal/ Spring_2011/Distracted_by.pdf. Accessed 4 Dec. 2019.

chapter 9

APA DOCUMENTATION

*He is wise who knows the sources of knowledge—who knows
who has written and where it is to be found.*
> ~ A. A. Hodge

WHEN DO YOU NEED TO USE APA RATHER THAN MLA?

Put simply: When your professor tells you to. Most paper assignments that
require research will tell you which documentation format to use. In the
social sciences (psychology, sociology, anthropology, etc.), it's APA (American
Psychological Association). Other disciplines, such as business, criminology,
nursing, linguistics, and economics also tend to use APA. When in doubt, of
course, ask your professor.

WHEN DO YOU NEED TO DOCUMENT?

You need to document your source any time you use an idea or piece of
information that is not yours. Important: This remains true even when you put
the information in your own words.

You don't need to cite "common knowledge," which includes strictly factual
information that can be found in a number of different sources. See page 115.

AS WITH MLA, DOCUMENTATION IN APA IS A TWO-STEP PROCESS.

Within your paper, provide a brief citation (in parentheses) of your source; then, on the "reference list" page (we called this a "works-cited page" in MLA), provide the detailed information about your source. There are other similarities between the two systems, but many, many, small differences.

IN-TEXT CITATIONS

When I say "in-text," I mean *your* text, the paper you're writing. For the examples here, pretend that these are sentences you would write in your paper. Pay attention to punctuation, spacing, and formatting.

In the social sciences, great value is placed on how recent the research is; as a result, the in-text citation will always include the year of publication.

BASIC FORMAT

Most of the time, your citation will look something like this:

Participants in online communities can be separated into two

groups: disclosers and listeners (Crawford, 2009).

(AUTHOR LAST NAME, YEAR OF PUBLICATION)

If you want to name the source in the sentence, use a signal phrase (the APA calls this a "narrative citation"):

SIGNAL PHRASE

According to Crawford (2009), participants in online

communities can be separated into two groups: disclosers and

listeners.

Papers written in APA format should use paraphrase and summary more than quotation, but you will occasionally want to quote a source. When you do, you should include the page number in your citation if one is available:

> As Crawford (2009) observed, "Listening is not a common metaphor for online activity" (p. 526).

If you don't use a signal phrase, it should look like this:

> As one researcher has observed, "Listening is not a common metaphor for online activity" (Crawford, 2009, p. 526).

Important: No matter how you identify the "source" (usually the author), it must correspond with a reference list entry; in other words, you must have a reference list entry that begins with **Crawford**.

VERB TENSES

Note that when using a signal phrase you should use past tense or present perfect tense: *Crawford found*, or *Crawford has found*. Again, this is in contrast to MLA guidelines, which call for almost all references to be in present tense.

TWO AUTHORS

Use the ampersand (&) between names when it's a parenthetical citation:

> In contrast to their older counterparts, young adults tended to be more careful in managing their online identities (Madden & Smith, 2010).

HOWEVER: If you refer to the authors in a signal phrase, use the word *and* rather than the ampersand:

> Madden and Smith (2010) found that young adults tended to be more careful in managing their online identities than their older counterparts.

THREE OR MORE AUTHORS

Provide the name of the first author and *et al.*, followed by the year.

> Social media sites such as blogs, photo-sharing sites, Wikis, and similar sites were estimated to be responsible for one third of all new Internet content (Finin et al., 2008).

OR:

> Finin et al. (2008) found that social media sites such as blogs, photo-sharing sites, Wikis, and similar sites were responsible for one third of all new Internet content.

Note: You'll need to name all the authors (up to 20) on the reference list page at the end of your paper.

NO AUTHOR LISTED / AUTHOR UNKNOWN

This will happen most commonly when you're citing a reference work, such as an encylopedia, that doesn't name individual authors of articles. Use the entire title of the source if it is short; if it's longer, use a shortened form. Put it inside quotation marks. The following example is from an *Encyclopædia Britannica* article about Twitter:

> The site has also been effectively used to raise money for a variety of causes; after the Haiti earthquake in 2010, Twitter users helped the Red Cross raise more than $8 million in just two days ("Twitter," 2012).

Note: How you abbreviate the title is up to you, but be sure to use the first word (unless it's *a, an* or *the*)—because this is the word a reader would be looking for on the reference list page. Also, make sure the comma is inside the quotation marks.

CITING TWO OR MORE WORKS AT THE SAME TIME

If more than one source has made a similar (or identical) observation, cite all the sources. This adds to the reader's perception of you as a thorough researcher.

Here's an example from the article by Kate Crawford used earlier:

> "Speaking up" has become the dominant metaphor for participation in online spaces such as blogs, wikis, news sites and discussion lists (Karaganis, 2007; Bruns, 2008).

A SOURCE WITHIN A SOURCE

In other words, imagine that you're reading an article by Crawford. In the article, Crawford uses Nick Couldry as a source, and you want to make reference to Couldry's idea. First, use a signal phrase to name the author whose idea you're using (Couldry, in this case); then, in a parenthetical reference, provide the information about the source where you read Couldry's idea.

> Nick Couldry cited reciprocity and embodiment as two distinct advantages of aurality (as cited in Crawford, 2009).

Note: APA discourages the use of these "secondary sources" in your paper.

Note: Your reference list should have an entry for Crawford, not Couldry.

SOURCES WITHOUT PAGE NUMBERS

Many non-print sources will not have page numbers; some will include paragraph numbers, and if they do, you should include this information after the date:

> In contrast to the older counterparts, young adults tend to be more careful in managing their online identities (Madden & Smith, 2010, para. 4).

If the paragraphs aren't numbered, use section headings:

> In 2008, a teenage girl sent a nude photo to her boyfriend, which he forwarded to many other students at her high school, leading to his expulsion from (Common Sense Media, 2010, Why sexting matters).

LONG QUOTATION (ALSO KNOWN BLOCK QUOTATION)

If you quote something that is 40 words or longer, format it as follows. See Appendix pages 217-221 for instructions on how to do the formatting.

1 While others describe lurkers as passive, Kate Crawford (2009) examined their behavior from a different perspective:

> **2** Listening has not been given sufficient consideration as a significant practice of intimacy, connection, obligation and participation online; instead, it has often been considered as contributing little value to online communities, if not acting as an active drain on their growth. (p. 527) **3**

4 This reconceptualizing of lurking leads to new ways of thinking about what it means to participate in an online community.

1 Your writing should introduce the quotation; use the author's name in this sentence and end with a colon (:).

2 Next is the block quotation, indented an additional 1/2 inch from your left margin. (See pages 217-221 for how to do it the right way.) Don't change the right margin. Double-space the block quotation just as you do the rest of your text. Don't use quotation marks.

3 If you're using a source with page numbers, put it at the end of the block quotation, inside parentheses, after the final punctuation mark.

4 Your writing after the block quotation should comment on what you just quoted.

Note: If you don't want to cite the source in the sentence, add it to the block quotation. In the example above, the end of the sentence would look like this:

growth. (Crawford, 2009, p. 527)

PERSONAL COMMUNICATION

If you interviewed someone or communicated with a source via email, telephone, or other electronic means, use the person's first initial and last name, along with the words *personal communication* (not in italics) in your citation. This guideline also applies to personal letters. Note: You do not need a reference list entry for these sources.

> According to T. Michaud (personal communication, January 18, 2020), the rules for psychological experiments using college students as subjects have changed dramatically over the last twenty years.

ORGANIZATION OR GROUP AS AUTHOR

If your source doesn't list a specific person as an author, you should use this guideline. The first time you cite the source, use the entire organization name; if you cite it again, use an abbreviation. If you only cite it once, don't include the abbreviation.

> As of 2019, 91% of 8- to 18-year-olds had a smartphone (Common Sense Media [CSM], 2020). CSM also reported that companies must ask for parental permission to sell any information from a child under the age of 16.

Or, for a single reference to the source:

> Common Sense Media (2020) reported that 91% of 8- to 18-year-olds have a smartphone.

REFERENCE LIST ENTRIES

FIRST, SOME UNIVERSAL GUIDELINES

CAPITALIZATION OF BOOK AND ARTICLE TITLES

Yet again, APA has very different rules from MLA. (APA is easier in this regard.)

Always capitalize   the first word of the title

the first word of a subtitle

proper nouns (names, monuments, etc.)

Do *not* capitalize   anything else

Examples:

Reputation management and social media

Following you: Disciplines of listening in social media

Celebrities and social influence: Identification with Elvis Presley

CAPITALIZATION OF JOURNAL NAMES

Always capitalize   first and last words; all the important words

Do *not* capitalize   prepositions, articles (unless they start the title)

Examples:

Abnormal Psychology

Journal of Medical Internet Research

The International Journal for the Psychology of Religion

ITALICS: NEEDED VS. NOT NEEDED

Generally, a work that stands alone (meaning: is not a part of something larger) will be italicized.

Always italicize   journal titles (see previous examples)

volume numbers (but not issue numbers) of journals

book titles

web pages

QUOTATION MARKS: NEEDED VS. NOT NEEDED

You will almost never need to use quotation marks on your reference list page; the only exception is if the title of an article or book you use has quotation marks within *its* title—in that case, put whatever the title has in quotes inside *single* quotation marks in your reference list entry.

AUTHOR NAMES: ONE, TWO, OR MANY

Always begin with the author's last name, followed by initial(s) for first name and middle name (if available). If you use two initials, type a space after the period following the first initial. Use an ampersand (&) rather than the word *and* before the final name. When you have multiple authors, you list all of them last-name-first:

One author: Smith, D. G.

Two authors: Smith, D. G., & Philips, J. T.

Three to twenty authors: Smith, D. G., Philips, J., & McBride, B. Q.

21 or more authors: List the first 19 authors as you usually would, then type an ellipsis (three periods, with spaces between each), and then the final author name (with no ampersand):

Smith, D. G., Philips, J., McBride, B. Q., Walcott, T., Diaby, A., Oxlade-Chamberlain, A., . . . Vermaelen, T.

ABBREVIATIONS OF MONTHS

Unlike MLA, APA does not abbreviate months; write them all out.

ABBREVIATIONS OF PUBLISHERS' NAMES

If the publisher is listed as, for example, The Macmillan Company, you would simply write Macmillan. However, keep the words *Press, Association,* and *Books* when they are part of the publisher name, e.g., University of Chicago Press.

SPACES

With some of the examples on the following pages, it's hard to tell where you should have a space. You always have a space after any mark of punctuation (comma, period, colon, semi-colon); also rememember that between each "part" of an entry (like, for example, between a magazine name and its date of publication), you always need a space.

DATABASE URL ADDRESSES

If you're using a library database, do not include the URL in your entry. Instead, use the DOI (digital object identifier; see next page for more info) if it's available. If not, simply end your reference after the page range.

RETRIEVAL DATES

APA recommends *not* including retrieval information, but if you think it's likely the URL will change, then you can include it. Also, check with your professor.

Retrieved February 10, 2020, from https://xxxxx

HANGING INDENT

Reference list entries should use a hanging indent—see Appendix pages 219-221 for how to format it.

CITATION GENERATORS

In most databases, you'll find a "citation generator," a tool that will give you a (mostly correct) reference entry for the source you're using. See Appendix pages 215-216 for more information.

INTERNET AND DATABASE SOURCES

BASIC FORMAT

Author last name, Initials. (Year). Title of article. *Title of journal, volume number*(issue number), pages. DOI or URL.

- Journal articles will often include a "DOI," or digital object identifier. It's a bit like a URL, but it's almost entirely numbers—and it's designed to never change (unlike many website URLs). If you can find the DOI, include it at the end of the entry as shown on the next page.
- If you can't find a DOI, use the URL (website address)—but don't use this if you found the source in a database.
- Note how the journal's volume and issue are written: volume *23* is italicized, but the issue number (4) and its parentheses are not. Also be aware that there's no space between those two elements.

ARTICLE IN A JOURNAL

Format: Abstract ▾   **KEY PUBLICATION INFO**   Send to ▾

J Soc Psychol. 2011 Mar-Apr;151(2):121-8. doi: 10.1080/00224540903365588. — **DOI**

Playing prosocial video games increases the accessibility of prosocial thoughts.
          ARTICLE TITLE

Greitemeyer T[1], Osswald S. — **AUTHORS**

⊕ Author information

Abstract
Past research has provided abundant evidence that playing violent video games increases aggressive tendencies. In contrast, evidence on possible positive effects of video game exposure on prosocial tendencies has been relatively sparse. The present research tested and found support for the hypothesis that exposure to prosocial video games increases the accessibility of prosocial thoughts. These results provide support to the predictive validity of the General Learning Model (Buckley & Anderson, 2006) for the effects of exposure to prosocial media on social tendencies. Thus, depending on the content of the video game, playing video games can harm but may also benefit social relations.

Greitemeyer, T., & Osswald, S. (2011, March–April). Playing prosocial video games increases the accessibility of prosocial thoughts. *Journal of Social Psychology, 151*(2), 121-128. https://doi.org10.1080/00224540903365588

Note: If there's no issue number, remove the (2) (including the parentheses).

Note: The title of the journal (top left of the image above, underlined) is abbreviated as J Soc Psychol; if you're not sure what the full title is, look for another version of the article so you can verify you have the full title.

ARTICLE IN A MAGAZINE OR NEWSPAPER ONLINE

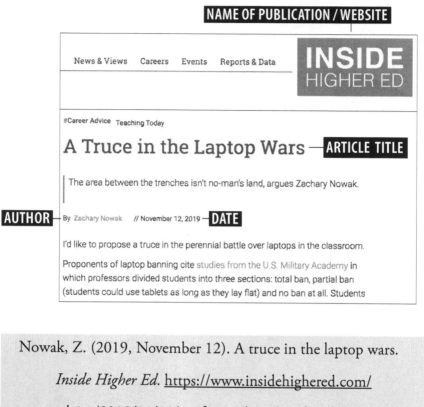

NAME OF PUBLICATION / WEBSITE

News & Views   Careers   Events   Reports & Data

INSIDE HIGHER ED

#Career Advice   Teaching Today

A Truce in the Laptop Wars — ARTICLE TITLE

The area between the trenches isn't no-man's land, argues Zachary Nowak.

AUTHOR — By Zachary Nowak   // November 12, 2019 — DATE

I'd like to propose a truce in the perennial battle over laptops in the classroom.

Proponents of laptop banning cite studies from the U.S. Military Academy in which professors divided students into three sections: total ban, partial ban (students could use tablets as long as they lay flat) and no ban at all. Students

Nowak, Z. (2019, November 12). A truce in the laptop wars. *Inside Higher Ed.* https://www.insidehighered.com/advice/2019/11/12/professor-describes-fruitful-compromise-allowing-laptop-use-class-opinion

ONLINE PAGE PUBLISHED BY GROUP OR ORGANIZATION

With most websites produced by an organization, the name of the organization itself can be listed as the author. Obviously, if there's a person's name listed as the author, use it.

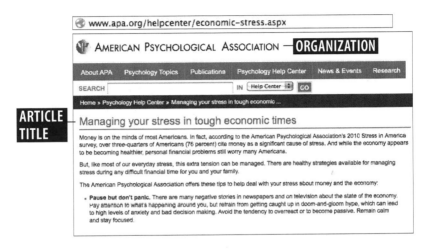

American Psychological Association. (2010). Managing your stress in tough economic times. https://www.apa.org/helpcenter/economic-stress

Note: I found the date by scrolling to the bottom of the page.

YOUTUBE / VIMEO / ONLINE VIDEO

This video appeared on YouTube. Most of the information you need is under the video itself, though sometimes you need to click on **Show More**.

Creative Genius: You | Patti Dobrowolski | TEDxBend — **TITLE | AUTHOR**

82,450 views · Jul 11, 2017 — **DATE OF PUBLICATION**   ↗ SHARE   ≡₊ SAVE   ...

TEDˣ   **TEDx Talks** ✓
23.1M subscribers

Everyone has a dream, but many people find it difficult to start, persist and remain focused long enough to achieve what they desire. In this compelling illustrated talk, Patti Dobrowolski, visual thinker and change activator, makes a bet with you that you can achieve your dreams by

SHOW MORE

Dobrowski, P. (2017, July 11). Creative genius: You. *YouTube*.

https://www.youtube.com/watch?v=zTZjAk6yqfY

BOOKS

Where to find key publication information:

- Title, subtitle, and author name will be on the cover of the book, obviously, though sometimes the formatting is unusual, in which case you're better off looking at the title page.

- The title page is usually the first "real" page of the book, or soon after. The publisher's name is almost always there. The spine of the book usually has the publisher's name too.

- The year of publication will be on the copyright page, after the © symbol.

BOOK WITH ONE AUTHOR

Author's Last Name, Initials. (Year of publication). *Book title: Book subtitle*.* Publisher.

* Include subtitle after a colon, and always capitalize the first word after the colon.

Pollan, M. (2006). *The omnivore's dilemma: A natural history of four meals.* Penguin.

BOOK WITH AN EDITOR

The editor is listed as the "main" author for the sake of the reference list entry. Keep in mind, though, that if you cite particular articles from within this book, you need an entry for each of these authors too. Yes, this is a little confusing. See next entry for how to cite a specific article (or two) from a book with an editor.

Noor Al-Deen, H. S. & Hendricks, J. A. (Eds.). (2012). *Social media: Usage and impact.* Lexington Books.

Note: If there is only one editor, the abbreviation would be (**Ed.**).

PART OF A BOOK WITH AN EDITOR / WORK IN AN ANTHOLOGY

If you found an article in a book that has other articles by different authors, this is how you document the article you're using.

The following book was edited (meaning: all the articles were selected by the editors) by Hana S. Noor Al-Deen and John Allen Hendricks. I want to cite one of the articles in the book; it's about Twitter in college classrooms, by Alec R. Hosterman. Start your entry with the author of the article; then, give the year of publication and the article title. *Then*, cite the editor and name of the book, starting with the word *In*, followed by page range of article.

> Hosterman, A. R. (2012). Tweeting 101: Twitter and the college classroom. In H. S. Noor Al-Deen & J. A. Hendricks (Eds.), *Social media: Usage and impact* (pp. 93-110). Lexington Books.

TWO OR MORE BOOKS BY SAME AUTHOR

Unlike MLA, you don't need to do anything differently here. Simply cite each book completely.

BOOK BY AN ORGANIZATION OR GROUP

Start with the name of the organization or group, followed by the date, and the book title.

> American Psychological Association. (2009). *Publication manual of the American Psychological Association* (6th ed.). American Psychological Association.

BOOK THAT LISTS AN EDITION

Many books (textbooks, especially) are republished with the same title but new content. If your book has an edition listed, it will probably be noticeable on the cover and/or the spine. In the reference list entry, put the edition after the title.

Briggs, A., & Burke, P. (2010). *Social history of the media: From*

Gutenberg to the internet (3rd ed.). Polity.

BOOK(S) IN MORE THAN ONE VOLUME

If the book you're using is part of a number of volumes, your citation should specify this.

Castells, M. (2009). *The rise of the network society: The information*

age: Economy, society and culture (Vol. 2). Wiley-Blackwell.

BOOK WITH NO AUTHOR

Don't write Anonymous or Anon. for the author. Just go straight to the title.

Primary colors: A novel of politics. (2006). Random House.

SAMPLE PAPER (APA)

See Appendix pages 214-223 for formatting in Word and Google Docs.

Margins: 1 inch on all sides. Indent all paragraphs 1/2 inch using TAB key or automatic indentation; don't use the space bar. Leave your right margin "ragged" rather than fully justified.

Spacing: Double-space everything, including block quotations and the reference list page.

Acceptable fonts (typefaces):

> serif fonts: 12-point Times New Roman, 11-point Georgia, or normal (10-point) Computer Modern (the default font for LaTeX)

> sans serif fonts: 11-point Calibri, 11-point Arial, or 10-point Lucida Sans Unicode

Many professors have specific requests for fonts—check the assignment.

Page number: It should appear on every page in a header in the top right corner. See Appendix pages 222-223 for how to format it.

TITLE PAGE

Title: Put it in **bold**, centered, starting about 1/3 down from the top of the page. Ideally, your title would fit on one line, but if you need two lines because you're using a colon, do it as it's shown on the next page.

Include one extra (double-spaced) line after the title.

Your name and course information: No bold for any of these elements.

Your name

Department, Name of College

Course Title: Name of Course

Professor (or Doctor) First Name Last Name

Date (don't abbreviate names of months here)

1

The Lure of the Device:

Why College Classrooms Need Less Technology

Jacob Smith

Department of English, Holyoke Community College

English 101: Composition I

Professor Fred Cooksey

March 6, 2020

Note: This essay was not written by a student, but by the author of this book, Fred Cooksey. See my explanatory note about why I did this on page 152.

The pages you see here are not to scale. In a Word document, the essay was 5.5 pages (1520 words), not including the title page or reference page.

2

The Lure of the Device:

Why College Classrooms Need Less Technology

Escaping the world around us is easier—and more

entertaining—than ever before. Most Americans have forgotten

what it feels like to be bored because we always have a phone,

laptop, or tablet nearby tempting us with amusing videos, streaming

sports, tweets, news, art, and just about anything else a human

might want to look at. These diversions are particularly alluring to

students in college classrooms, it seems. As a result, most professors

have a policy regarding use of devices in the syllabus. Some take

a relaxed approach, either because they have given up trying to

enforce stricter policies, or because they truly believe in the benefits

of students having access to a variety of technological tools in the

classroom. Other professors argue that a complete prohibition

is necessary both for their own focus while teaching and for the

protection of students who might be distracted by their peers' use of

1 Repeat your full title here, again in bold. Don't skip any extra lines after it.

2 The introduction starts with a broader issue—technology's effect on all of us—before it narrows into the more specific subject of this paper.

3/4 These sentences offer summaries of the two main positions on the issue.

3

phones and laptops. Neither extreme offers a compelling solution,   5
but much of the evidence now suggests that both students and
professors would benefit from limiting the use of devices in the
classroom.

A prominent argument in favor of allowing laptops in the   6
classroom is that students can take notes more effectively on
a laptop, thus allowing them to retain and review classroom
information more effectively. Advocates for note-taking on a laptop
argue that most students can type far more quickly than they can
write by hand; it seems logical that this would result in better
learning. In order to understand recent research that examines
the effect of laptops on note-taking and learning, it is useful to
understand what happens when people take notes. In the early
1970s, Francis Di Vesta and Susan Gray (1972, as cited in Mueller   7
& Oppenheimer, 2014) found that the connection between note-
taking and learning had two components, "encoding" and "external
storage." Encoding is what happens while the person is taking notes,

---

5   Thesis statement comes after the comma—and it's in the right place here at the
end of the introduction.

6   This topic sentence clearly announces exactly what this paragraph will
explore—a naysayer (see page 80) in the overall argument.

7   This is the correct way to cite a "source within a source." See also page 166.

4

when the brain is processing what the note-taker hears and sees. External storage is what happens when the person tries to recall the information later, as for example on an exam. The distinction is important because it could reveal more about the differences between taking notes by hand versus on a laptop.

Recent research does, in fact, suggest that taking notes by hand [8] results in better retention of material. Mueller and Oppenheimer (2014) conducted three experiments involving note-taking by hand [9] versus on a laptop. They found that when students took notes on a laptop—in the "encoding" phase of learning—they were not processing the information well because they tended to rely on "verbal transcription" (p. 8). In other words, they were simply [10] typing what they heard rather than thinking about the information. By contrast, students who took notes by hand were forced to be more selective about what they wrote down, leading to a higher level of processing. When subjects in their study were tested a week after the initial note-taking exercises, those who had used laptops

---

8 Topic sentences don't have to be overly elaborate; simple can be effective.

9 Always use past-tense verbs ("conducted") when citing research in APA.

10 If you worked from a PDF, you should have a page reference; use it. Also on that line: If you write "In other words" after a quotation, it forces you to restate or explain the source material—always a good idea.

5

"performed worse on tests of both factual content and conceptual

understanding, relative to participants who had taken notes

longhand" (p. 8).

11

A follow-up study from the United States Military Academy

(also known as West Point) found that poor student performance

was not merely the result of how students took notes, but that

the presence of the devices themselves seemed to be the problem.

Payne Carter et. al. (2016) compared the results of students in

introductory classes who could freely use devices at any time

with two other groups, one that had a complete prohibition on

all devices, and another that could use tablets. The researchers

concluded that "computer devices have a substantial negative

effect on academic performance" (p. 128). They also hypothesized

that the differences in performance they found might be greater

at other institutions, primarily because West Point is one of the

most selective universities in the country—and students there are

extremely motivated to perform at a high level. Glass and Kang

(2019) came to similar conclusions as the researchers at West Point.

Interestingly, they found that students performed equally well

11   Many professors don't want you to end a paragraph with a quotation. It's not ideal here, but at least it makes a good connection to the next paragraph.

6

on in-class assignments whether they were using devices or not. However, when they measured student performance on unit exams and final exams, they saw statistically significant worse outcomes: Students who did not use any devices received an average score of 87 on final exams, while those who had used devices scored just 80.

Not everyone views the issue of distraction as a problem, however. Many students appear to know that they might not perform quite as well if they are distracted; still, they argue that they should still have the right to engage in these behaviors because they only hurt themselves, not others in the class. Other students claim that texting during class can actually improve their focus. They describe it as "just like . . . doodling" and contend that it "helps me listen better" (Williams et al., 2011, p. 54). More significantly, though, many students argue that when college lectures are unengaging, students should be free to do what they like during class, particularly if they are not disturbing other students. Students have justified texting during class, for example, by saying, "I'm not learning anyway" and "I text because I'm bored, so I was not

12

12 Again, this is a relatively simple but effective topic sentence. Note the use of the transitional word *however*, which helps alert the reader that the writer is again presenting the views of a naysayer.

7

learning to begin with" (Williams et al., p. 54-55). There does   13

appear to be legitimacy to these complaints, and this connects with

one of the more positive developments related to the controversy

over the use of devices: Many colleges have been actively trying

to help faculty develop more engaging ways of delivering their

material—so that students will pay attention.

For many professors, though, the key issue is not whether   14

individual students are giving the professor their full attention;

instead, they are concerned that one student's use of a device can

be distracting to *other* students. Sana et al. (2013) reported that

students "in view of multitasking peers scored significantly lower

on the test than [those] not in view of multitasking peers" (p. 29).

In other words, students did worse on tests when they could see

another student who was distracted. A student in another study put

it succinctly: "I get distracted by them being distracted" (Williams

et al., 2011, p. 53). Glass and Kang (2019) found this to be true

---

13   If you use the same source twice in the same paragraph, which is the case here, you don't repeat the year in your citation.

14   This is a more complex topic sentence. It makes a good transition from the previous paragraph by restating the basic idea from that paragraph (students not giving their full attention) and also uses the transitional word *though* to alert the reader that this paragraph will go in a different direction.

8

in their research as well: "Performance on the unit exams and final exams was poorer for students who did not use electronic devices during the class as well as for the students who did use an electronic device" (p. 404). Again, the evidence shows that it is not just the student using the device whose learning suffers; other students nearby are affected as well. Furthermore, in their observations of the classroom itself, Glass and Kang noted that when students "tried to direct attention to the instructor, there was distracting activity on both sides and in front of them" (p. 404). Given these adverse effects on other students, it seems clear that professors should reconsider policies that allow students too much freedom in terms of their use of devices during class.

15

One potential solution also addresses the issue of students with disabilities. By law, professors must allow students with documented disabilities certain "accommodations," and one of the most common is a laptop for note-taking. If a professor has a ban on laptops in the classroom but one student is clearly using one,

16

15 The final sentence of this paragraph makes a key point not just for this paragraph but for the paper as a whole.

16 The paper introduces an entirely new issue here—students with disabilities—and I think this is a good place for it because it also explores a possible solution that is neither a complete ban or complete permissiveness.

9

then other students in the classroom will know that that student has a disability. This is an unacceptable and unethical breach of that student's right to privacy. One professor, however, has a clever and seemingly effective solution to this problem; Zachary Nowak (2019) banned laptops in his classroom, but made two exceptions to the ban:

17

> Anyone who had an accommodation could use one, as could anyone who came to my office hours and made a case for why they wanted to use one during class. I expected a number of students to select the second option and decided I would set a relatively low bar but would ask those students to sign a contract that outlined how they would use the laptops during class.

The result was that no students requested to use a laptop, thus protecting the privacy of the students with disabilities who did use them. Nowak describes the resulting classroom atmosphere as

18

---

17 If you have a quotation that is 40 words or longer, use a block quote. The entire block quote is indented 1/2 inch from the left margin; the right margin stays the same. The first line of the block quote is never indented. See page 167 for how to do it and pages 217-221 for how to format it.

18 This is where you should explain and/or comment on the information in the block quote. Because this sentence continues the ideas of the paragraph before the block quote, it isn't indented. Effectively, it's all one paragraph.

10

"palpably less distracted." It might not be a perfect solution, but given the complexities of the issue, Nowak's approach is one that many professors should consider.

When cell phones first became popular in the 1990s, arguments   19 would occasionally develop about the etiquette of having a phone conversation in public. Those disputes are rare now, of course, though clearly we are still learning how these devices will be part of our social—and educational—lives. College is a place where learning and growth are supposed to happen, so perhaps we should trust that eventually the college classroom will evolve in ways that make today's difficulties with technology seem like a minor and temporary blip. Until that time, though, it seems wise for students—voluntarily or otherwise—to resist the undeniable lure of the device and be fully present with their classmates and professors. They may actually learn more and perform better as a result.

19 There's no need to start your final paragraph with "In conclusion," "In summary," or something similar. Remember too that you don't simply restate what appeared in your introduction. This should say something slightly new while re-asserting your thesis. This conclusion uses a common technique for the final part of a paper: It looks forward and makes a recommendation.

11

References

[20] Carter, S. P., Greenberg, K., & Walker, M. (2017). The impact of
computer usage on academic performance: Evidence from
a randomized trial at the United States Military Academy.
Economics of Education Review, 56, 118–132. https://doi.
org/10.1016/j.econedurev.2016.12.005

Clayson, D. E., & Haley, D. A. (2013). An introduction to
multitasking and texting prevalence and impact on grades and
GPA in marketing classes. *Journal of Marketing Education.*
35(1), 26-40. https://doi.org/10.1177/0273475312467339

Glass, A. L., & Kang, M. (2018). Dividing attention in the
classroom reduces exam performance. *Educational Psychology.*
39(3), 1-14. https://doi.org/10.1080/01443410.2018.148904

Nowak, Z. (2019, November 12). A truce in the laptop wars.
Inside Higher Ed. https://www.insidehighered.com/
advice/2019/11/12/professor-describes-fruitful-compromise-
allowing-laptop-use-class-opinion

---

[20] Continue the double spacing on the reference page(s). Learn how to format the "hanging indent" on page 219-221.

12

Sana, F., Weston, T., and Cepeda, N. J. (2013, March). Laptop multitasking hinders classroom learning for both users and nearby peers. *Computers & Education. 62*, 24–31. https://doi.org/10.1016/j.compedu.2012.10.003

Williams, J. A., Berg, H., Gerber, H., Miller, M., Cox, D., Votteler, N., & McGuire, M. (2011). "I get distracted by their being distracted": The etiquette of in-class texting. *Eastern Educational Journal, 40*(1), 48-56. https://castle.eiu.edu/edjournal/Spring_2011/Distracted_by_their_distracted.pdf

chapter 10

STUDENT PAPERS

Knowing a great deal is not the same as being smart; intelligence is not information alone but also judgment, the manner in which the information is collected and used.

~ Carl Sagan

This chapter contains two student papers. Unlike the papers at the end of Chapters 8 and 9, these really were written by students. Both follow MLA documentation guidelines.

Kyle Wright: "New Collar Workforce: Catalysts for Change in the Workplace"

1475 words, 5.5 pages, not including works-cited pages

Sophia Boardway: "Industrial Agriculture: America's Provider of Food"

1050 words, 3.5 pages, not including works-cited page

Comments on Sophia's paper by her professor, Christopher Kobylinsky

Kyle Wright

Professor Cooksey

English 101.29

6 December 2012

New Collar Workforce:

Catalysts for Progressive Change in the Workplace

As the Millennial generation, a cohort with dates of birth

ranging from the 1980s to early 2000, enters the workforce, analysis

surrounding this new generation attempts to uncover just what

this digitally native, feedback-driven demographic has to offer. As

this demographic begins to gain distinction from its predecessor

Generation X, these young people will have a significant impact

on the modern workplace. Many generational analysts insist

that Millennials lack disciplinary traits needed in the workplace.

Professionalism, structure, and management skills are common

shortcomings of this demographic, according to a survey conducted

by Adecco, a human resources consulting firm (Bednarz). Of

course, it is true that many of the characteristics of Millennials clash

with the traditional work environment; however, the Millennial

generation will ultimately transform the outdated workplace into

one that fosters efficiency, productivity, and flexibility. Replacing

Wright 2

expectations of conventional structure and adherence to process,
this modern take on the workplace is one that promotes and
properly utilizes this generation of assertive and refined workers—a
generation of born entrepreneurs.

Numbering at around sixty million and representing ten
to fifteen percent of the workplace, Millennials are poised to
be powerful drivers of the economy, both as employees and as
consumers (Bannon et al.). Employers must work to meet the
needs of Millennials entering the workplace, including flexibility,
compensation, and opportunity. In turn, the characteristics of the
Millennial generation will come to meet the needs of the business,
redefining the workplace and creating a symbiotic relationship
between employee and employer that will promote efficiency,
results, and balance for both sides of the working relationship.

Stretching Our Legs: A Focus on Flexibility   1

In a recent study conducted by MTV, 79 percent of Millennials
thought that they should be allowed to wear jeans to work,

---

1   Kyle uses section headings in this paper, which can help the reader see the
organization of your paper more clearly—but they are no substitute for good
transitions. Also, some professors may not want you to use section headings,
so check first.

compared to only 60 percent of Baby Boomers (Miller). While dressing for comfort rather than professionalism may be an insignificant fashion change, it may indicate a much larger trend of freedom and flexibility in the workplace. Dan Schawbel, a Gen Y career expert and the founder of Millennial Branding, argues that this change toward a flexible and often casual work environment is caused by the Millennial generation's desire for a deeper work-life integration. Unlike previous generations, Millennials don't talk about balancing work and life, but rather about blending them.

Work-life balance is a growing concern for the Millennial generation, who refuse to work long hours at the expense of their personal life. According to the Pew Research Center, when asked to rate how important various life goals were to them, Millennials ranked being a good parent as a top priority, and the importance of the family outranked fame and fortune (Bannon et al.). Life goals such as parenting and spending time with the family may cause Millennials to challenge the conventional nine-to-five workday in favor of a flexible schedule that allows for better integration of their personal and professional lives (Bannon et al.). To create a balance between a productive career and a healthy lifestyle, the Millennial generation's redefined workplace emphasizes quality of work

Wright 4

over number of hours and success over a structured adherence to schedule.

A few companies—Best Buy, I.B.M., and Capital One   2
Financial Corporation—have begun to embrace the Millennial desire for a healthy and flexible work-life balance in radical and exciting ways. Best Buy human resource managers Cali Ressler and Jody Thompson have developed the Results-Only Work Environment, or ROWE. This program offers employees complete control over their time, so long as their work gets done. As Ressler and Thompson explain in their book *Why Work Sucks and How to Fix It*, "A true ROWE has unlimited paid vacation time, no schedules, no mandatory meetings, and no judgments from co-workers and bosses about how employees spend their days" (61). Instead of rewarding employees on how many hours they log or how well they navigate office politics, ROWE advocates say that a relentless focus on results forces managers to be clear about expectations, allows employees to create a work life balance that is right for them, and increases productivity while reducing cost and employee turnover rates.

2   Note the uses of dashes to set off information that might have been confusing if Kyle had used commas, primarily because the three companies named here need commas between them. For more on dashes, see page 89 - 91.

Wright 5

Even at Best Buy headquarters, however, ROWE isn't 3 universally accepted. Tyler Shaw, a Best Buy employee and participant in the ROWE program, acknowledges, "There are some people who feel hostile about ROWE and want to continue micromanaging" (qtd. in Alsop 171). Managers voice concerns about this radical movement, perceiving it as an attempt by employees to get away with getting paid for "slacking off" (Barr). Telecommuting and working remotely have been around for years, but little evidence is available to show that these changes do much more than improve employee satisfaction and eliminate commutes. Shaw encourages his colleagues to look at ROWE from an economic perspective: "People spend their time like money, and time has power because it is a limited, nonrenewable resource. People spend their time in the most efficient manner possible to get the desired outcome." Through the implementation of a Results Only Work Environment, companies have boosted both economic results and employee morale. After migrating to a ROWE, departments at Best Buy reported productivity increases of 35 percent (Blakely). In addition, Best Buy's Strategic Sourcing and

3   Note the excellent transition Kyle has created here. It works well because the first few words pick up on the ideas from the previous paragraph, and the word *however* lets you know that he's shifting in a different direction.

Wright 6

Procurement Team boosted employee retention by 27 percent, and saw a 50 percent increase in cost reductions over two years.

The Ambitious Generation

Raised in a world surrounded by breakthrough advancements—the boom of the internet, social media networks, and mobile computing—the Millennial generation has become synonymous with ambition, a trait that defines a born entrepreneur. This ambition, and the many ways it benefits the symbiotic relationship between the business and the Millennial, is a dominant factor driving change in the redefined workplace.

While many Millennials are not driven to succeed by a fancy title or the corner office, this generation is interested in how their contribution to the workplace will make a positive difference. As John Spano, a human resources director for a movie theatre company, observes, "If you expect them to stand behind a register and smile, they're not going to do that unless you tell them why that's important and then recognize them for it" (qtd. in Twenge 217). Regardless of position or rank in the

4

4   Kyle's source (Jean Twenge) was quoting her own source, John Spano; Kyle handles the "quoted in" construction perfectly. See pages 121-122 for more information.

Wright 7

company hierarchy, Millennials' ambition will drive them to make suggestions to improve the work environment. Although this may seem disrespectful of authority, businesses should recognize these suggestions as contributions to the symbiotic relationship between employer and employee; managers should reciprocate by offering reasonable opportunity to pursue these ambitions "not by wearing a colorful T-shirt on a special project once a year, but [through] their actual work" (Miller). If managers properly utilize the ambition of this generation they can unleash the potential of "all that mobility and access to information" (Miller), and can build a diverse, networked, and transparent work environment.

5

Some argue, however, that the ambition of the Millennial generation does not always bring positive change to the workplace. As sociologist and Millennial critic Jean Twenge observes, "The optimism of youth, combined with the instant gratification that technology has provided, often leads to impatience" (219).

6

5   Note the use of square brackets here to indicate that Kyle has changed this word; for more on how/when to do this, see page 122.

6   Kyle provides a clear **topic sentence** for this paragraph; this sentence plainly states what Kyle will be doing now: exploring some complications to the argument he has been making. We call these competing voices naysayers (see page 80). Using language like "Some argue" is an excellent way to force yourself to recognize competing perspectives.

Wright 8

Some young people will enter the workplace with unrealistic expectations of promotions, or see their career development process as a zigzagging line that allows them to jump around the company hierarchy at their leisure. "This is especially true of the most qualified young people," explains Twenge, "[who] have been encouraged to have lofty ideas about their future" (219). In this situation, both parties must be reasonable about basic expectations in the workplace. While a company may provide flexibility in terms of time management, "employees control . . . how hard they work" 7 (Alsop). If aiming for senior management positions, Millennials should be aware that they are going to have to work hard, often putting in long hours and travel. On the other hand, recruiters promising flexibility may mislead Millennials into believing they can work where and when they want from day one of an entry-level position, when in reality these flexible options may only be available to a small group of experienced employees.

7   The ellipses (. . .) here indicate that Kyle has left out words from the quotation, which originally read, "employees control the throttle on how hard they work." See page 124 for more information on when and why to use ellipsis marks.

Wright 9

Looking Forward

In the coming years, due to the retirement of baby boomers [8] and the relatively smaller size of Generation X, corporations will find Millennials to be in high demand in the job market. As the workplace changes, companies will need to consider how they "attract, retain, and leverage the future of our workforce" (Bannon et al.). Employers looking to unlock the potential of a generation of born entrepreneurs must work to embrace Millennial characteristics and utilize generational talents and skills. By creating a flexible work-life balance and harnessing the ambition that motivates this generation, businesses and Millennials can foster the symbiotic relationship that brings a fresh look and new energy to the working environment, while encouraging this generation of emerging leaders to continue driving positive change in the workplace.

[8] Kyle's conclusion wraps up the paper nicely. He only uses one source here, which is appropriate—you want to make sure that *yours* is the dominant voice in the conclusion. The concluding sentences reveal his voice and his view on the subject, but these are not merely a restatement of the introduction; instead, he looks slightly beyond the scope of the current thinking on the subject to offer predictions about the future of Millennials in the workplace.

Wright 9

Works Cited

Adams, Susan. "Older Workers, There's Hope: Study Finds
   Employers Like You Better Than Millennials." *Forbes*, 24 Sept.
   2012, www.forbes.com/sites/susanadams/2012/09/24/older-
   workers-theres-hope-study-finds-employers-like-you-better-
   than-millennials/#16b390cd4aa6. Accessed 8 Nov. 2012.

Alsop, Ronald. *The Trophy Kids Grow Up: How the Millennial
   Generation Is Shaking Up the Workplace.* Jossey-Bass, 2008.

Bannon, Shele, et al. "Understanding Millennials in the
   Workplace." *CPA Journal*, vol. 81, no. 11, 2011,
   pp. 61-65. *Academic OneFile.* search.proquest.com/
   openview/c7d2cc4ebea1c9d5be5d2768b9421384/1?pq-
   origsite=gscholar&cbl=41798. Accessed 12 Nov. 2012.

Barr, Corbert. "Why Doesn't Everyone Work in a Results-Only
   Work Environment (ROWE)?" *Think Traffic*, 31 May 2009,
   corbettbarr.com/why-doesnt-everyone-work-in-a-results-only-
   work-environment-rowe/. Accessed 8 Nov. 2012.

Bednarz, Ann. "Hiring Preferences Favor Mature Workers
   over Millennials: Study." *Network World*, 9 Oct. 2012,
   www.networkworld.com/article/2160554/infrastructure-
   management/hiring-preferences-favor-mature-workers-over-
   millennials--study.html. Accessed 20 Nov. 2012.

Wright 10

Blakely, Lindsay. "What Is a Results-Only Work

    Environment?" *CBS News*, 25 Sept. 2008, www.cbsnews.

    com/8301-505125_162-51237128/what-is-a-results-only-

    work-environment. Accessed 2 Dec. 2012.

Conning, Denise, and Devika Cook. "Bridging the Generational

    Divide in the PACU." *The Dissector: Journal of the Perioperative*

    Nurses College of the New Zealand Nurses Organization, vol.

    40, no. 1, 2012, pp. 27-36. *Academic OneFile*. connection.

    ebscohost.com/c/articles/84198826/bridging-generational-

    divide-pacu. Accessed 27 Nov. 2012.

Miller, Matt. "Why You Should Be Hiring Millennials." *Forbes*, 3

    July 2012, www.forbes.com/sites/mattmiller/2012/07/03/why-

    you-should-be-hiring-millennials-infographic/#72ef8f4a37f8

Ressler, Cali, and Jody Thompson. *Why Work Sucks and How*

    to Fix It: The Results-Only Revolution. Portfolio/Penguin,

    2011. *Google Books*, books.Google.com/books/about/Why_

    Work_Sucks_and_How_to_Fix_It.html?id=dVK9ROrsDL0C.

    Accessed 4 Dec. 2012.

Twenge, Jean M. *Generation Me: Why Today's Young Americans Are*

    More Confident, Assertive, Entitled—and More Miserable Than

    Ever Before. Free Press, 2006.

Boardway 1

Sophia Boardway

Professor Kobylinsky

English 101.25

16 December 2019

Industrial Agriculture: America's Provider of Food

Industrial agriculture or factory farms are responsible for   1

producing the majority of the meat, eggs, and milk Americans

consume on a daily basis. From the 1700-1800s, Americans raised   2

animals in open spaces or as free-range. Due to overgrazing and

weather-related issues, traditional farming methods were no longer

enough to sustain the growing need for more food and taken

over by federal control. As demands grew and lands needed to

support them decreased, livestock were relocated into extensive

factory farms, which were large industrialized indoor farms that

maximized the production of food at minimum cost. Treatment of

pigs, cows, and chickens inside these concentrated animal feeding

operations (CAFOs) lead to cruel management of livestock, overuse

of antibiotics and massive amounts of toxic waste that pollutes

1   Sophia introduces the essay's topic in the first sentence.

2   Sophia gives brief but essential context (over the next four sentences) to the
essay's topic prior to the thesis.

Boardway 2

our environment. Therefore, industrial agriculture uses inhumane   3
methods to mass-produce food for the overconsumption habits of
Americans today, creating health-related issues in the livestock and
people consuming them and pollution of the environment.

Industrial agriculture uses antibiotics as a tool to increase the   4
rate of CAFOs animal's growth and to treat them preventatively,
producing dangerous bacteria. Livestock living inside factory
farms are kept confined in small stalls in close proximity to each
other, making the spread of bacteria rapid. Producers put profit
over treatment and constantly feed the animals with low-dose
antibiotics to increase the number of products produced. According
to Jennifer Weeks, "Swine, poultry, and beef cattle producers   5
use from 16 million to 27 million pounds of non-therapeutic
antibiotics on animals every year." Non-therapeutic antibiotics
are used by farmers for reasons other than disease prevention in
livestock. Antibiotics should only be used when there's a medical

---

3   The thesis statement takes a clear stance on the issue, setting up the rest of the
     paper to provide a logical, detailed argument to justify that stance.

4   The body paragraph's topic sentence establishes a narrowly focused claim that
     develops and defends one aspect of the thesis statement.

5   Sophia provides credible and informative textual evidence through facts and
     figures.

Boardway 3

need, not to increase growth. The living conditions of CAFOs are

unclean due to waste management issues and constant confinement,

causing high levels of stress, which can weaken the animal's immune

systems. According to Weeks, "Big livestock operations also give

animals antibiotics as a preventative, because by raising only a few

selected breeds their animals have less natural genetic protection

against disease, and sickness spreads easily in close quarters. Stress

from overcrowding also lowers animals' resistance." Even though

antibiotics are used to increase production, they also interact

with bacteria, leading to a type of bacteria with drug-resistance.

Drug-resistance in bacteria is caused by constant over exposure to

antibiotics. The altered bacteria become drug-resistant, multiply and

continue to spread diseases to the compromised immune systems

of CAFO animals. These animals are becoming dependent on the   6

presence of antibiotics in their diets to manage illnesses that go

along with living in confinement. Antibiotics as a tool to promote

growth and reproduction rates is unnatural and inhumane. The

presence of drug-resistant bacteria remain in animals after slaughter

and production and are ultimately consumed by people. The

6   Through analysis, Sophia draws connections between what she gathered from
the source and her own stance on the issue.

Boardway 4

CAFOs producing food generate emissions from both the factories   7
and the animals inside them.

Emissions and waste from animals held inside of CAFOs   8
generate methane and could be responsible for rises in greenhouse
gas emissions, leading to global warming. Global warming is
caused when the earth's atmosphere traps heat from the sun,
rising temperatures and affecting the environment. An increase
in livestock produced major amounts of methane, which is a
greenhouse gas like carbon dioxide. Maanvi Singh reports that
"in 2011, methane from livestock accounted for 39% of all the
greenhouse gas emissions from agriculture... methane from
livestock rose 11% between 2001 and 2011." The amount of
food Americans eat has increased over the last decade, increasing
the amount of methane produced. The animal's digestive process
contributes to higher levels of methane from the food they consume
that is filled with antibiotics and hormones. Large CAFOs contain
1,000 or more cows, pigs, and chickens that contribute to the
rising methane and nitrous oxide greenhouse gases that escape

7 Sophia transitions between paragraphs.

8 Sophia uses specific wording to establish the paragraph's claim, avoiding
general or vague statements.

into the environment (Singh), leading to further pollution of the environment.

CAFOs are unsustainable because they risk the health of our environment from a pollution point of view. Since livestock are held in factory farms, their manure is washed out of the barns and held in "lagoons" until used as fertilizer for crops. A single dairy cow produces 22 tons of manure every year and a CAFO can produce 500 million tons of waste a year (Weeks). According to Weeks, "The stored, liquefied manure can leak or be washed away by big storms, contaminating nearby waters with bacteria, hormones, nutrients, antibiotics, and toxic chemicals." The contaminants are washed away by rain, draining into rivers and even drinking water supplies, spreading diseases and countless other harmful substances to other animals and people. According to Eliza Barclay, "Overconsumption of red meat... is linked to health epidemics like diabetes and cancer . . . ." This link may be caused by the unnecessary amount of antibiotics and hormones farmers use in the meat production process and the use of contaminated manure as fertilizer on our crops. Since the demand for more food requires more livestock, factory farms are increasing in size, but they are few and far between. This means the larger the CAFO, the more manure

Boardway 4

they are producing, leading to even more pollution in the already compromised environment.

Industrial agriculture uses inhumane methods to mass-   9 produce food for the overconsumption habits of Americans today, causing issues not only with the animals and people that consume them but the environment as well. Americans generally don't ponder where their food originates from, so a deeper understanding of industrialized farms would benefit our society and make us conscious of our choices. Factory farming isn't sustainable, but it has changed to fulfill the needs of the growing population of America without thinking of the effects it has on the sustainability of our environment. For a process to be sustainable,   10 it has to be economically viable, socially equitable, and protect the environment. Industrial agriculture is economical and socially equitable but it's not protecting the environment, it is harming it. Factory farms provide America with meat, eggs, and milk

---

9   At the beginning of the conclusion, Sophia brings the essay full circle by rephrasing the thesis statement. Now that she has proven her argument in the body paragraphs, she is essentially saying to her reader, *See? I told you so.*

10   In the final sentences of the conclusion, Sophia looks at the "larger picture" of her topic.

Boardway 5

with unsustainable methods. Industrial agriculture isn't the most sustainable way to mass-produce food, but produces are noticing the mismanagement of this system and are working on sustainable solutions.

Boardway 5

Works Cited

Barclay, Eliza. "Why Farmers can Prevent Global Warming Just as
    Well as Vegetarians." *NPR,* 25 Feb. 2014, https://www.npr.
    org/sections/thesalt/2014/02/24/282117840/why-farmers-
    can-prevent-global-warming-better-than-vegetarians.

Singh, Maanvi. "Gassy Cows are Warming the Planet and They're
    Here to Stay." *NPR,* 12 Apr. 2014, www.npr.org/sections/
    thesalt/2014/04/11/301794415/gassy-cows-are-warming-the-
    planet-and-theyre-here-to-stay.

Weeks, Jennifer. "Factory Farms: Are They the Best Way to
    Feed the Nation?" *CQ Researcher,* 12 Jan. 2007, library.
    cqpress.com.ezproxyhcc.helmlib.org/cqresearcher/getpdf.
    php?id=cqresrre2007011200.

Comments by Christopher Kobylinsky

When I discuss with students how to structure a college essay, I first share with them a quote from Ernest Hemingway: "Prose is architecture, not interior decoration."

Why does this matter to students writing college essays? Many students transitioning from high school to college feel the need to write "academically." That is, to use multisyllabic words culled from a thesaurus, or to web together complex syllogisms of thought, or to (in effect) sound "collegiate."

The truth about writing academically, however, is quite the opposite: it is, essentially, to take a complex idea and present it to a reader as clearly as possible. And where or how do you begin doing this? Structure. As the Hemingway quote suggests, in order to convey meaning to a reader, you first have to worry about structuring sentences and paragraphs that will best convey that idea with clarity.

Most of that "sounding academic" stuff is really just interior decoration. Rugs, curtains, and pictures do not hold a house up—the foundation, beams, walls, and ceilings do. Once you figure out and master the basic structure of an essay—the architecture of it—writing a paper becomes much more straightforward, and you can more easily begin to take a complex idea and lay it out logically, sequentially, and clearly.

* * *

In Sophia's paper, you can see that she has mastered the basic formula for structuring the essay. Her opening paragraph introduces the topic, provides essential context for that topic, and then offers a thesis. Each body paragraph, likewise, follows its own formula: topic sentence, details, textual evidence, analysis, concluding remark, and transition to the next paragraph. Finally, the conclusion brings the essay full circle by rephrasing the thesis and leaving the reader with "larger picture" remarks about the topic. By following these steps, the student has a structure on which to build her thesis.

Yes, formulas are meant to be bent, twisted, and broken, but as you begin to write essays for the first time at the college level, see if you can first master the basic structure of an essay.

appendix

TECHNOLOGY TIPS

Getting information off the internet is like taking a drink from a fire hydrant.

~ Mitch Kapor

DON'T LOSE THAT FILE—SAVE IT TO THE CLOUD

I have computers at home and at work, and a laptop, and a phone. Thanks to Dropbox, I can work on a file at home, give it a moment to sync, and then find the updated version on my two other computers and my phone.

Many sites offer cloud storage, but Dropbox is well established and strikes me as very secure. Still, you should take normal precautions with any personal information you store in the cloud.

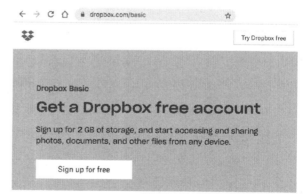

Note: They don't make it easy to find your way to the **free version** of Dropbox; you can search *Dropbox free* or try the URL above: <u>dropbox.com/basic</u>

Google Docs works the same way, and there is an option for working offline, though you have to use the Chrome browser for it to work.

USING A CITATION GENERATOR

If you use a library database for research, you'll find that many of the databases offer a "citation generator." See page 115 for directions to generate a citation from a database article; the button is at the bottom right in this image:

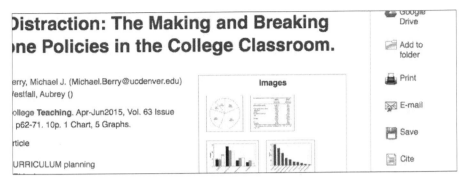

After you click the Cite button, the next screen will show you many different citation styles, starting with ABNT (never heard of it). You'll need to scroll down to MLA or APA.

Citation Format

NOTE: Review the instructions at EBSCO Connect and make any necessary corrections before using. **Pay special attention to personal names, capitalization, and dates.** Always consult your library resources for the exact formatting and punctuation guidelines.

ABNT (Brazilian National Standards)	References BERRY, M. J.; WESTFALL, A. Dial D for Distraction: The Making and Breaking of Cell Phone Policies in the College Classroom. **College Teaching**, [s. l.], v. 63, n. 2, p. 62, 2015. DOI 10.1080/87567555.2015.1005040. Disponivel em: http://search.ebscohost.com.ezproxyhcc.helmlib.org/login.aspx?direct=true&db=f5h&AN=102498739&login.asp&site=ehost-live&scope=site. Acesso em: 24 fev. 2020.
AMA	Reference List

The easiest way I've found to do this is to copy the entry here and paste it into a Word document (or Google Docs) and then fix the formatting.

MLA (Modern Language Assoc.)	Works Cited Berry, Michael J., and Aubrey Westfall. "Dial D for Distraction: The Making and Breaking of Cell Phone Policies in the College Classroom." *College Teaching*, vol. 63, no. 2, Apr. 2015, p. 62. *EBSCOhost*, doi:10.1080/87567555.2015.1005040.

When you paste it, be sure to choose the option "Match Destination Formatting." This way, it will have the same formatting as the rest of your paper. But there will still be a few elements to fix.

> Berry, Michael J., and Aubrey Westfall. "Dial D for Distraction: The Making and Breaking of Cell Phone Policies in the College Classroom." *College Teaching*, vol. 63, no. 2, Apr. 2015, p. 62. *EBSCOhost*, doi:10.1080/87567555.2015.1005040.

The most common problem with these citations (epecially when you copy-paste them) is that you lose the hanging indent. See next pages for how to do this correctly. By the way, I recommend that you wait until you have all your sources on your works-cited page and then do the double-spacing and hanging indent all at once.

Another problem here is that the page numbers are not correct; the entire arcticle was not just on page 62. From the first image on the previous page you can see that the pages are 62-71, so I'll fix that too. Check everything by comparing your entry to the appropriate example from Chapter 8 or 9. In this case, you'd want to look at page 135.

> Berry, Michael J., and Aubrey Westfall. "Dial D for Distraction: The Making and
>
> Breaking of Cell Phone Policies in the College Classroom." *College Teaching*, vol.
>
> 63, no. 2, Apr. 2015, pp. 62-71. *EBSCOhost*, doi:10.1080/87567555.2015.1005040.

Here's the APA version, which also needed the capitalization of the title fixed. Check it against the example on page 173.

> **APA** (American Psychological Assoc.)
>
> References
> Berry, M. J., & Westfall, A. (2015). Dial D for Distraction: The Making and Breaking of Cell Phone Policies in the College Classroom. *College Teaching*, *63*(2), 62. https://doi-org.ezproxyhcc.helmlib.org/10.1080/87567555.2015.1005040

> Berry, M. J., & Westfall, A. (2015). Dial D for distraction: The making and breaking of
>
> cell phone policies in the college classroom. *College Teaching*, *63*(2), 62-71.
>
> https://doi-org.ezproxyhcc.helmlib.org/10.1080/87567555.2015.1005040

FORMATTING A BLOCK QUOTATION AND HANGING INDENT

Block Quotation in Microsoft Word

There are a couple of ways to do this, but I think the easiest is to use the ruler, which you can find under the View menu if it's not already visible. Start by highlighting the part that you're putting in the block quotation.

This is an unacceptable and unethical breach of that student's right to privacy. One professor, however, has a clever and seemingly effective solution to this problem; Zachary Nowak banned laptops in his classroom, but made two exceptions to the ban:

Anyone who had an accommodation could use one, as could anyone who came to my office hours and made a case for why they wanted to use one during class. I expected a number of students to select the second option and decided I would set a relatively low bar but would ask those students to sign a contract that outlined how they would use the laptops during class.

The result was that no students requested to use a laptop, thus protecting the privacy of the students with disabilities who did use them. Nowak describes the resulting classroom atmosphere as "palpably less distracted."

Here's a close-up of the controller on the left side of the ruler and the three most common settings you'll use.

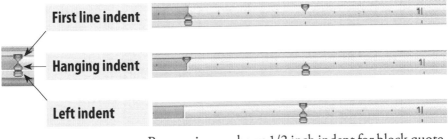

Bottom image shows 1/2 inch indent for block quote.

This is what it should look like once you've shifted the block quote 1/2 inch to the right. Make sure the next paragraph doesn't get indented since that should be where you follow up on what you've quoted.

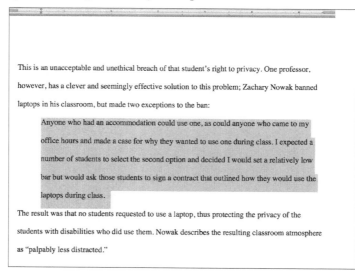

If you're having trouble with the ruler, use the **Format** menu to go to **Paragraph** settings; there, set the Left indentation at 0.5" and under the word Special, choose **(none)**.

Hanging Indent in Microsoft Word

Again, using the ruler is the easiest way to do this. Also, I recommend that you do all your works-cited entries at the same time. Go back two pages to see the close-up of the ruler controls.

BEFORE:

Berry, Michael J., and Aubrey Westfall. "Dial D for Distraction: The Making and Breaking of Cell Phone Policies in the College Classroom." *College Teaching*, vol. 63, no. 2, Apr. 2015, pp. 62-71. *EBSCOhost*, doi:10.1080/87567555.2015.1005040.

AFTER:

Berry, Michael J., and Aubrey Westfall. "Dial D for Distraction: The Making and Breaking of Cell Phone Policies in the College Classroom." *College Teaching*, vol. 63, no. 2, Apr. 2015, pp. 62-71. *EBSCOhost*, doi:10.1080/87567555.2015.1005040.

If you're having trouble with the ruler, use the **Format** menu to go to **Paragraph** settings; there, under the word Special, choose **Hanging**.

Block Quotation in Google Docs

Again, using the ruler is the easiest way to do this. If it's not already showing, use the **View** menu to choose **Show ruler**. Then, drag the bottom part of the controller in the ruler 1/2 inch to the right:

laptops in his classroom, but made two exc

Anyone who had an accommodatic

office hours and made a case for w

number of students to select the se

bar but would ask those students to

laptops during class.

The result was that no students requested

students with disabilities who did use them

atmosphere as "palpably less distracted."

If you're having trouble with the ruler, use the **Format** menu to go to **Align & indent** settings, then choose **Indentation options**.

See settings on next page.

Format Tools Add-ons Help All changes saved in Drive

Text ▶

Paragraph styles ▶

Align & indent ▶

Line spacing ▶

Columns ▶

Bullets & numbering ▶

Headers & footers

Page numbers

Table ▶

Image ▶

Clear formatting ⌘\

Borders & lines ▶

≡ Left ⌘+Shift+L

≡ Center ⌘+Shift+E

≡ Right ⌘+Shift+R

≡ Justified ⌘+Shift+J

≡ Increase indent ⌘+]

≡ Decrease indent ⌘+[

Indentation options

Set the **Left indentation** at 0.5" and under **Special indent**, choose **(None)**.

Hanging Indent in Google Docs

You can use the ruler for this, but it's a two-step process: First, drag the bottom part of the controller 1/2 inch to the right, then drag the top part back to zero so that it looks like this:

Berry, Michael J., and Aubrey Westfall. "Dial D for Distraction: The Making and Breaking of Cell Phone Policies in the College Classroom." *College Teaching*, vol. 63, no. 2, Apr. 2015, pp. 62-71. *EBSCOhost*, doi:10.1080/87567555.2015.1005040.

If you're having trouble with the ruler, see the directions at the bottom of the previous page to get to the **Indentation options**. There, use the **Special indent** menu to choose **Hanging**, and then enter .5 in the field beside it.

INSERTING A PAGE NUMBER (AND YOUR NAME) IN A HEADER

In Microsoft Word

Under the **Insert** menu, choose **Page Numbers**. On the next screen, choose **Top of page (Header)** as shown below and **Right** for Alignment. Check the box marked **Show number on first page**, then click **OK**.

If you're writing a paper in APA format, you're done—because you don't need to add your name. But if you're writing a paper in MLA format, double-click to the left of the page number. This will open the header. Type your last name and be sure to hit the space bar before the number:

INSERTING A PAGE NUMBER (AND YOUR NAME) IN A HEADER

In Google Docs

Under the **Insert** menu, let your cursor hover over **Page numbers**, then choose the image showing page numbers in the top right corner of the page.

| Insert | Format | Tools | Add-ons | Help |

- Image ▶
- Table ▶
- Drawing ▶
- Chart ▶
- Horizontal line
- Footnote   ⌘+Option+F
- Ω Special characters
- π² Equation
- Headers & footers ▶
- Page numbers ▶
- Break ▶
- Link   ⌘K
- Comment   ⌘+Option+M
- Bookmark

Choose this one.

If you're writing a paper in APA format, you're done—you don't need to add your name. But if you're writing a paper in MLA format, double-click to the left of the page number. This will open the header. Type your last name and be sure to hit the space bar before the number, then hit ESC or click anywhere else in your text to exit the header.

Smith 1

Header   ☐ Different first page   Options ▾

Professor Cooksey

English 101.15

6 December 2019

Let the Students Type (and Text, and Shop):

College Classrooms Need to Embrace Student Use of Technology

Index

A

Abbreviations of months
 APA 171
 MLA 131
Academic journals. *See* Scholarly journals
Active reading 25
Active voice 20
Analytical writing 78–80
Anthology
 citation (APA) 178
 citation (MLA) 146–147
 in-text (MLA) 125
APA Documentation
 In-text citations 162–166
 Reference list entries 169–188
  Abbreviations 171
  Author names: one, two, or many 170
  Citation generators 172–173
  Italics: needed vs. not needed 170
  Quotation marks: needed vs. not needed 170
  Spaces 171
Artwork
 citation (MLA) 151
Author names, one or more
 citations (APA) 170
 citations (MLA) 130
 in-text (APA) 163–164
 in-text (MLA) 119
Author, none listed
 in-text (APA) 165
 in-text (MLA) 120

B

Block quotation 123, 217
   how to format in Google Docs 220–221
   how to format in Word 217–218
   in your paper (APA) 167
   in your paper (MLA) 123
Blog post, works cited 136
Books
   citations (APA) 177–179
Brackets 122, 200
Brainstorming 69

C

Capitalization
   citations (APA) 169
   citations (MLA) 129
   proper nouns 52
   title of your paper 51
Changing the wording of quotations 122
Citation generators 110
   how to format 215–216
Comma splice 39
Conclusions 202
Conjunctive adverbs 41
Course packet
   citation (MLA) 148
Critical thinking 25, 27

D

Databases 106–111
Database sources
   citation (APA) 172
   citation (MLA) 134–135
Dependent words 40
DOI 172
Drafting an essay 77–78
Dropbox 214

E

E-book. *See* E-reader
Ellipses 124, 201
E-reader
  citation (MLA) 144
  in-text (MLA) 128
Ethics of writing 21
Ethos, pathos, logos 22

F

Fake news 16
Film / DVD, citation (MLA) 150
First person 81
Fragment 41
Freewriting 69

G

Google Scholar 104–105
Google searches 96–103
Government agency, citation (MLA) 137–138

H

Handout, citation (MLA) 148
Hanging indent 131
  how to format in Google Docs 221
  how to format in Word 219

I

Informative vs. argumentative writing 11–12
Internet sources
  citation (APA) 172
  citation (MLA) 132
In-text citations (APA) 162–168
In-text citations (MLA) 116–126
iPad. *See* E-reader
"I" statements. *See* First person

J

Journalist 13

K

Kindle. *See* E-reader

L

Letter of reference (request) 8
Library books, finding 112–113
Long quotation. *See* Block quotation
Long titles, citation (MLA) 130

M

Margins of your paper
 (APA) 180
 (MLA) 152
MLA Documentation
 In-text citations 116–126
 Works-cited entries 129–153
Months
 abbreviate (APA) 171
 abbreviate (MLA) 131

N

Naysayer 29, 80, 155, 183, 186, 200
Nook. *See* E-reader

O

Organization or group as author
 citation (APA) 175
 citation (MLA) 138
 citation of book (APA) 178
 citation of book (MLA) 145
 in-text (APA) 168
 in-text (MLA) 125

P

Page numbers, adding to your paper
  Google Docs 223
  Microsoft Word 222
Page numbers, in-text citations
  (APA) 163
  (MLA) 118
Paraphrase 58–59
Passive voice 20
Peer-reviewed publications 19
Plagiarism 59, 64
Podcast
  citation (MLA) 140
  in-text (MLA) 128
Primary vs. secondary sources 56
Pronoun reference "errors" 44
Proofreading 93–94

Q

Quotation marks vs. italics
  (APA) 170
  (MLA) 50–51
Quoting a source 59–60
Quoting vs. paraphrasing 61

R

Radio program
  citation (MLA) 140
  in-text (MLA) 128
Recommendation letter request 8
Reference list entries. *See* APA Documentation
Reporter 13
Revision 82

S

Saving your work 214
Scholarly journals 18
  citation (APA) 173
  citation (MLA) 135
Scholars 14
Section headings in your paper 195
Signal phrases 55–62, 117
Spaces
  citations (APA) 171
  citations (MLA) 131
Spacing of your paper
  (APA) 180
  (MLA) 152
Spell Check, dangers of 94

T

TEDTalk
  citation (MLA) 142
Television show
  citation (MLA) 150
Thesis statement 74–75
They as singular pronoun 44
Titles
  Capitalizing title of your paper 51–52
  Long titles. *See* Long titles
  Quotation marks vs. italics. *See* Quotation marks vs. italics
Topic
  Finding 68
  Narrowing 69
  vs. thesis 74
Topic sentences 77–78, 154, 184, 187, 200
Transcript. *See* Radio program
Transfer application 8
Transitions
  Between paragraphs 82–83, 198
  Between sentences 83
Twitter
  citation (MLA) 139

V

Vague language 87–88
Video / Vimeo / Online video
  citation (APA) 176–179
  citation (MLA) 141–142

W

Works-cited entries. *See* MLA Documentation

Y

YouTube. *See* Video

Made in the USA
Middletown, DE
13 August 2023

36599160R00133